SCHOLASTIC

THE ULTIMATE BOOK OF
PHONICS WORD LISTS
FOR GRADES 3-5

Word, Phrase, and Sentence Lists, Plus Games
for Reading, Writing, and Word Study

LAURIE J. COUSSEAU AND RHONDA GRAFF

DEDICATION

To Joann Crawford, my mentor who taught me everything
I know about linguistic structure and who transformed
the lives of so many children and educators
— L. C.

To Craig, Dan, Genna, and Abbi, with love …
so proud of you all
— R. G.

Thank you to our editor, Maria Chang,
for her support and guidance.

SVP & Publisher: Tara Welty
Editor: Maria L. Chang
Creative director: Tannaz Fassihi
Cover design: Cynthia Ng
Interior design: Maria Lilja
Images © Shutterstock.com and The Noun Project.

ISBN: 978-1-5461-1365-2

Scholastic Inc., 557 Broadway, New York, NY 10012
Copyright © 2024 by Laurie J. Cousseau and Rhonda Graff
Published by Scholastic Inc. All rights reserved.
Printed in the U.S.A.
First printing, April 2024.

1 2 3 4 5 6 7 8 9 10   40   30 29 28 27 26 25 24

CONTENTS

INTRODUCTION

"Teaching reading is rocket science."
–Louisa Moats, Ed.D.

To teach children how to read requires a deep understanding of language and linguistics. Our brains are hardwired to speak and listen, but not to read or spell.

As teachers, reading specialists, literacy consultants, and Orton-Gillingham trainers, we have used various programs and methodologies to teach reading. We recognized the need for resources to help teachers teach foundational skills in reading and writing. We wanted to create an easy-to-use, comprehensive resource that supports structured literacy instruction based on the science of reading.

In the first two books of the Ultimate Book of Phonics Word Lists series (for Grades K–1 and 1–2), we covered foundational phonetic patterns, syllable types, and syllable division patterns. In this resource for Grades 3–5, we delve into another layer of linguistics—*morphology*, which includes beginning prefixes, roots, and suffixes. *Morph* is a bound root of Greek origin, meaning "form" or "shape." The suffix *-ology* means "the study of." While a *phoneme* is the smallest unit of sound, a *morpheme* is the smallest unit of linguistic meaning. This is a deep layer of language that is ideal for vocabulary instruction.

This resource can be used in a variety of settings—across the three tiers of instruction, in general education and special education programs, and for homeschooled children. It should be noted, however, that this is a resource, not a curriculum.

How to Use the Lists, Games, and Assessments

There are a multitude of morphemes to explore and learn. *The Ultimate Book of Phonics Word Lists for Grades 3–5* provides a useful entry into this layer of *etymology* (word origin) and vocabulary. We have chosen a useful selection of morphemes based upon common usage and organized around meaning. Having an understanding of word origin and the etymology of a morpheme contributes to a deeper understanding of the rules and patterns of our language. As students become discriminating linguists, English becomes increasingly accessible and logical. The word lists, phrases, and sentences were carefully chosen and organized to highlight these morphemes.

We created a flexible, teacher/parent-friendly resource. A teacher, specialist, or tutor can identify the prefixes, roots, and suffixes that will best serve a child, group of students, or class.

WHAT IS ENGLISH?

English has one of the most complex alphabetic and orthographic systems. The structure of the words help reveal their origin.

English as we know it was first brought to Brittania in the 5th and 6th centuries CE (Common Era). The Angles and Saxons migrated to Brittania, bringing continental words of Germanic origin. Anglo-Saxon was established by 600 CE. Britannia became known as "land of the Angles," which is now referred to as England.

Latin became infused into the English language during the Norman invasion in 1066. In the urban centers, French became the primary language for approximately 300 years. Anglo-Saxon was preserved in the outlying more rural pastoral areas.

Greek entered the English language during the Renaissance in the 16th century.

HISTORY OF ENGLISH

English is derived from many languages. The spelling and pronunciation of a word often unlock its etymology. For the purposes of this book, words are commonly divided between three influential languages: Anglo-Saxon, Latin, and Greek. Anglo-Saxon words make up approximately 20–25 percent of English words. These words are primarily one-syllable, basic vocabulary words, including colors, farming, body parts, and irregular words. The variability of the vowels makes these challenging for reading and spelling. Some examples include: consonant digraphs (*ch, th, sh, wh*), the spelling generalizations (*-ck, -tch, -dge*), the FLOSS pattern (*ff, ll, ss*), the basic six syllable types, vowel teams (e.g., *ai/ay, ee/ea, oa/ow, eigh, ough*), "kind old" words, silent-letter teams, inflectional suffixes (*-s, -ed, -ing*), and irregular sight words. A chart is provided for reference (see page 10).

Words of Latin origin make up approximately 55 percent of English words. Latin is composed of morphemes: prefixes, roots, and suffixes. Knowing the meaning of prefixes, roots, and suffixes opens up the knowledge of vocabulary in higher-level expository and narrative text. Latin words are longer, but the individual morphemes are highly decodable and recognizable. For example, prefixes can be open syllables (*re, pre, de*) and roots often having a short vowel (*rupt, dict, ject*). Latin words rarely have vowel teams, and *V-e* is more common (*recede*).

Greek words are often associated with literature, science, and the arts. Words of Greek origin are often characterized by *ch* as /k/, as in *chorus*; *ph* as /f/, as in *graph*; *sc* as /s/, as in *science*; medial *y*, as in *myth*; or *y-e*, as in *rhyme*. Greek words are estimated to make up 10 percent of English words. It can be helpful to compare the similar vocabulary words of Anglo-Saxon, Latin, and Greek origins. For example, compare the Anglo-Saxon word *star* with the Latin word *stellar* and the Greek word *astronomy*. Or explore the terms *earth, fire,* and *water* with the Latin words *terrain, ignite,* and *aquatic* and the Greek words *geographic, pyre,* and *hydrogen*.

WORD LISTS FOR READING

Choose the number of words for students to read based on each child's ability and their exposure to various morphemes and vocabulary. Be careful not to overload them.

You can present the words to students by writing them in columns, a grid, or on cards that can be stored for future use. Students can read up and down a column or across rows in a grid. If students' first pass at reading the words is not automatic, have them read the words again to help improve fluency. You may need to model the proper pronunciation or assist with supporting strategies, such as dividing a word by morphemes. For example, students can circle the prefix and/or suffix and isolate the root or underline the base word. Then students can read each part and blend them together. In addition, students can discuss the meaning of each morpheme and use that to identify the meaning of the word.

Whether using lists or cards, note how students are reading the words: correctly or correctly with automaticity. Also, take note of student errors so you can provide guided correction and plan accordingly. In a future lesson, revisit those words for students to reread. Continue to provide other words with a similar morphemic structure for further practice until the student no longer needs the review.

After students have read through the words, ask questions or use prompts to enhance vocabulary. For example:

- *What word means . . . ?*
- *What word is the opposite of . . . ?*
- *Find a synonym for . . .*
- *Use a word in a sentence.*
- *Use two words in the same sentence.*

For a cumulative review, include words from previously taught morphemes to create a mixed list. Additionally, plug the words into the game-board templates to supplement single-word reading and build vocabulary.

WORD LISTS FOR SPELLING

To build students' spelling skills, dictate words with the same morphemic pattern used in your reading lists. Include review words and words that students had trouble reading or understanding in prior lessons.

The number of words you dictate for spelling will depend on the student and may be fewer than the words provided for reading. Choose spelling words that are different from the words students have read but still follow the same morphological construction. Create a master list of reading and spelling words so you can record errors for an individual student or a small group.

When you dictate a word for students to spell, it may be helpful to have them repeat or whisper the word prior to writing it to engage the auditory track. Have students orally syllabicate the word and spell each syllable or morpheme, if needed. Make note of the affixes and roots. Discuss their meanings. Students now have options to tackle unknown words. The ability to unlock a longer decodable word, such as *interconnectedness*, is a powerful motivator for a struggling reader. If students had prior exposure to syllable division, they can transition to dividing a word by morpheme. For example, the word has five syllables (*in-ter-rupt-i-ble*) but three morphemes (*inter-rupt-ible*). Peeling back to the base word is also a helpful strategy. For example, take the word *unpublished*. If we take off the prefix *un-* and the suffix *-ed,* we

WORD STUDY

The root carries the primary meaning of the word. A **free root** can stand alone without a prefix or suffix. A **bound root** does not have meaning on its own unless an affix (prefix or suffix) is added.

Prefixes can be added to a word to change the meaning. Suffixes are either inflectional or derivational. **Inflectional suffixes** indicate grammatical features, such as number, person, tense, or comparative forms (*dogs, waits, walked, smaller*). **Derivational suffixes** add meaning or change the part of speech (*hope* to *hopeful*).

The word *re-tract-ed* is an example of a morphologically constructed word. The bound root *tract* means "to pull." The prefix *re-* means "back" or "again." The inflectional suffix *-ed* indicates past tense.

are left with the base word *publish*. Students feel empowered when they are able to read and understand the meaning of longer words.

Collect students' spelling lists and use an error analysis diagnostically. For instance, if a student makes a spelling error, such as "ficshun" (*fiction*) or "perheat" (*preheat*), use guided questioning to help the student understand the nature of the mistake. By looking at the errors students make, you can note areas of confusion and plan instruction accordingly.

Invite students to read back the spelling words as another pass at fluency.

When students learn the phonetic patterns, generalizations, and morphemic patterns, they no longer need to study words for a weekly spelling test. They can apply their knowledge and spell many words correctly without prior studying because of the depth of their understanding.

PHRASES AND SENTENCES FOR READING

Following each word list is a phrase and sentence list for each suffix, prefix, or root. Use these to promote oral reading fluency and to help students see how to use the words in context. The sentences can be "scooped" for phrasing.

Encourage students to read the sentences several times with increasing prosody. Feel free to modify or extend the sentences based on students' needs.

PHRASES AND SENTENCES FOR DICTATION

You can also dictate the phrases and sentences. Begin with a phrase or two, then dictate sentences in increasing length. Have students repeat the phrase or sentence prior to writing it on paper. You can expand the sentences orally so students are not limited by spelling. For example, you may wish to expand the sentence, "We went on vacation," to "Last summer, my family and I went on vacation to a lake house."

If students struggle to remember the sentence, have them repeat it a few times prior to writing it. Encourage them to cluster phrases and clauses and to visualize the sentence.

C – capitalization
H – handwriting
O – order of words
P – punctuation
S – spelling

Teach students the importance of rereading their work to check for accuracy by using the acronym CHOPS. Have students reread the sentence they wrote and check off each letter to see whether their sentence is accurate. Does it have capital letters where needed? Is it neatly written? Does it include all the words in the correct order? Is it correctly punctuated? Is every word correctly spelled? (A teacher may need to check the spelling.) This is a great way to reinforce important aspects of writing sentences.

Afterwards, have students read back their sentences for more practice with fluency.

VOCABULARY

An enriched vocabulary can improve understanding. Morphology naturally lends itself to vocabulary instruction. Students learn the meaning of each morpheme and can then extract meaning from new and unfamiliar words. The Simple View of Reading formula shows that reading comprehension is the product of strong decoding and strong language comprehension (Gough & Tunmer, 1986; Hoover & Gough, 1990).

Explore words in depth with students, helping them understand how to use the words in sentences. Note synonyms and antonyms, which are often formed by affixes (e.g., *hopeful/hopeless, likely/unlikely*). There are many opportunities for vocabulary exploration using the word, phrase, and sentence lists as a springboard. Also, consider using the word lists to create vocabulary cards that can be used for review. You can find a template online. (See below for more information on how to access the supplemental online resources.) Revisiting the words on multiple occasions in various ways helps students incorporate the words into their vocabularies.

GAMES

Included in this resource are 10 reproducible word games and activities that provide fun ways to reinforce the morphemic patterns. Customize the blank game boards to highlight any pattern or skill. Since all the games and activities require students to read words, we recommend that an adult be present to check for accuracy.

Use guided questioning to help students understand why they made a mistake and to help them fix it. Encourage students to explain the strategies, rules, and patterns they are using. For example, *Why do you double the final letter of a word when adding a vowel suffix? What part of speech is a word that ends in* -tion? Students develop a deeper understanding when they can explain why.

Make extra copies of each game to send home for practice and reinforcement.

ASSESSMENTS

Online, you will find informal progress-monitoring assessments for most of the skill levels in the book. Assessments for word reading, phrase reading, sentence reading, and spelling are included.

We also provide teacher record sheets to support good recordkeeping and anecdotal note-taking. Each teacher record sheet has space allocated for two different assessments— a pre- and post-test.

We have also included blank assessments and blank teacher record sheets along with detailed instructions for teachers and parents to customize their own assessments.

SUPPLEMENTAL ONLINE MATERIALS

In addition to the assessments, we also provide lists of function words, content words, and irregular words, and other useful resources online. To access these materials, go to **www.scholastic.com/phonicswordlists** and enter the password **SC766601**.

Teachers who are equipped with the understanding of etymology can enrich their lessons with information about the construction of words, their meanings, and their origins. We hope you enjoy using this resource as much as we enjoyed creating it!

Morphology Reference Chart

ANGLO-SAXON — 20%–25% of words in English

- Numbers: *one, two, five*
- Basic colors: *green, red, blue*
- Simple body parts: *arm, nose, throat*
- Irregular sight words: *said, was, could*
- Vowel teams: *boat, house, night*
- Silent-letter teams: *knee, write*
- Consonant digraphs **ch, th, sh, wh:** *chime, thin, ship, when*
- **ff, ll, ss, zz:** *cliff, spell, miss, buzz*
- **-ck, -tch, -dge:** *duck, patch, edge*

LATIN — 55% of words in English

- Words constructed with a prefix + root + suffix
- Soft **c** before **e, i, y:** *century, circular, cygnet*
- **ti, si, ci** /sh/: **-tion:** *fiction;* **-sion:** *mission, version;* **-cian:** *musician*
  -tial: *partial;* **-tious:** *cautious;* **-cient:** *ancient;* **-cious:** *gracious*

Roots can be grouped by meaning:

Body parts
- **ped** ("foot"): *pedestal*
- **tact / tang** ("touch"): *tactile*
- **man / manu** ("hand"): *manual*
- **dict** ("speak"): *prediction*
- **vis / vid** ("see"): *visionary*
- **spect** ("look"): *inspector*
- **aud** ("hear"): *audience*

Motion
- **rupt** ("break"): *eruption*
- **tract** ("pull"): *distraction*
- **port** ("carry"): *portal*
- **pend** ("hang"): *impending*

GREEK — 10% of words in English

- **ph** /f/: *sphere, photograph, dolphin, phosphate*
- **ch** /k/: *school, chorus, chaos, chord*
- **medial y** /i/: *gymnast, myth, mystery*
- **y-e** /ī/: *thyme, rhyme, lyre, pyre*
- **sc** /s/: *science, scent, scene*
- **k** in longer words: *kinesthetic, kilometer*
- **th** in longer words: *athlete, thyroid*
- **-ology:** *biology, geology, ornithology*

The Ultimate Book of Phonics Word Lists for Grades 3–5 © by Laurie J. Cousseau and Rhonda Graff, Scholastic Inc.

Suffixes and Inflectional Endings

Suffixes are attached to the end of a base word or root. *Suf* means "under or below," and *fix* means "to attach." Suffixes can be inflectional or derivational. Inflectional suffixes indicate grammatical features, such as number (e.g., *-s*, *-es*), tense (*-ed*, *-ing*), or comparative forms (*-er*, *-est*). Derivational suffixes add meaning to words or change their part of speech (for example, *hope → hopeful*).

Both kinds of suffixes are very useful for students to know as they provide readers with the ability to read longer words. We typically teach young students basic Anglo-Saxon suffixes—such as *-ed*, *-s/-es*, and *-ing*—early on. Over time, students learn Latin connective suffixes, such as *-tion* or *-ture*, which may have unexpected pronunciations, but are very useful for both reading and spelling.

Due to the nature of spoken English, the vowel in a suffix may also be pronounced with a schwa, as in the suffix *-ent* in the word *president*. It can be helpful to teach this articulation. As we switch from teaching students to divide a word into syllables to teaching them to divide a word into meaningful parts (morphemes), they will discover that a suffix can be more than one syllable, as in *-ology* or *-able*.

Students may also notice that the meaning of some endings is more concrete while others seem more abstract. Examples of suffixes with a clear meaning are *-ful* (meaning "full of," as in *hopeful*) and *-less* (meaning "without," as in *cloudless*). It will be useful for students to know these definitions. With a suffix like *-tion* (meaning "the quality of," as in *fiction*), the instructional focus can be on usage (noun) as the meaning is not as easily generalized. The suffixes featured in this book are not exhaustive, but we chose them for their high utility and usability.

Inflectional Suffix	Derivational Suffix

• Indicates grammatical features
  • Number (*dogs*)
  • Tense (*walked*)
  • Comparative forms (*smaller, largest*)
	• Adds meaning
	  (*hope → hopeful, hope → hopeless*)
	• Changes part of speech
	  (*wind → windy*)

-ed: happened in the past

The past-tense suffix -ed has three sounds: /ed/, /d/, and /t/.

- When a base word ends with the letter t or d, the -ed suffix is pronounced /ed/, as in planted or landed.
- When a base word ends with a voiced consonant (such as /g/, /l/, /m/, /n/, /ng/, /y/, or /z/), the -ed suffix is pronounced /d/, as in pulled or played.
- When a base word ends with an unvoiced consonant (such as /f/, /k/, /p/, /s/, or /t/) or ss, sh, x, or -tch, the -ed is pronounced /t/, as in fished or patched.

In some cases, when -ed is added to a word, its spelling might change. When adding the suffix to some words that end with a single consonant, the final consonant may be doubled, as in stopped. When adding a suffix to some words that end in final e, the e may be dropped, as in liked. However, we recommend beginning with words that require no spelling change to the base word, as in played or planted. **Note:** Words in shaded boxes are multisyllabic words that contain the highlighted ending.

-ed Words

-ed /ed/			
acted	hinted	sanded	distrusted
added	landed	shifted	expanded
banded	lasted	slanted	impacted
blasted	lifted	squinted	insisted
chanted	listed	stranded	intended
dented	melted	tended	invented
drafted	mended	tested	objected
drifted	painted	tilted	predicted
dusted	panted	trusted	prevented
ended	planted	twisted	recorded
folded	printed	waited	refunded
frosted	quilted	wanted	rejected
gifted	rented	consulted	responded
granted	rested	contacted	resulted
handed	rusted	contracted	suspected

The Ultimate Book of Phonics Word Lists for Grades 3–5 © by Laurie J. Cousseau and Rhonda Graff, Scholastic Inc.

-ed /d/			
banged	grilled	skilled	belonged
buzzed	learned	smelled	delivered
called	longed	spelled	enjoyed
clanged	mailed	spilled	prolonged
coiled	pinged	stayed	recalled
drilled	played	thrilled	refilled
filled	pulled	wailed	revived
filmed	rolled	winged	unskilled
fizzed	sailed	yelled	

-ed /t/			
asked	helped	pressed	tricked
backed	hissed	pumped	watched
brushed	honked	rocked	whacked
bumped	inched	sacked	whisked
camped	jumped	shocked	winked
cashed	licked	smashed	worked
checked	locked	sniffed	confessed
chirped	looked	soaked	detached
clashed	mashed	splashed	enriched
crunched	masked	stacked	finished
dressed	missed	stamped	published
dumped	packed	stuffed	unleashed
fished	passed	thanked	unlocked
fixed	picked	thumped	unmissed
flushed	pinched	trashed	unpacked

Inflectional Endings

-ed Phrases

rested and mended	called and yelled	jumped and landed
sanded and painted	banged and clanged	checked the tent
melted in the heat	refilled the glass	missed lunch
drifted on the river	stayed too long	brushed my long hair
looked under the bed	camped under the stars	acted and painted
soaked in the bath	spelled all the words	landed and fished
intended change	delivered package	unpacked the suitcase
frosted glass	granted a wish	invented a robot
buzzed and fizzed	sailed the seas	enjoyed the dance
stacked the logs	watched the race	published author

-ed Sentences

They sanded and painted the cabin.	They helped us to sail the boat.
We jumped off the boat to help.	We landed and fished, then sailed away.
The big sister lifted the baby from the crib.	We rolled and jumped on the bed.
The happy kids splashed in the pond.	My cousins stayed for the weekend.
The bubbles in the sink buzzed and fizzed.	The boat drifted lazily down the river.
We rested and drifted off to sleep after the long hike.	The hikers checked the tent before they slept.
The pans and pots banged and clanged when they were put back.	The gifted singers acted in the play and finished with a song.
She called and yelled, but we couldn't hear her across the lake.	We stacked the firewood and then grilled fish for dinner.
The unpacked suitcase sat in the living room for days!	The delivered package was left by the front door.
We were granted three wishes after opening the magical box.	Robert invented a robot that could do his homework.
We watched the race and cheered on the runners.	Paula is a published author, and she is only 10 years old.

The Ultimate Book of Phonics Word Lists for Grades 3–5 © by Laurie J. Cousseau and Rhonda Graff, Scholastic Inc.

-ing: happening in the moment

When attached to a base word and joined with a conjugated "to be" verb, the suffix *-ing* indicates an action is happening in the moment. (For example: *I was singing. I am singing. I will be singing.*)

When adding *-ing* to some words, we may have to double the final consonant (e.g., *stopping*) or drop the final e (e.g., *liking*). See pages 22–30 for the three spelling rules for adding suffixes. We recommend introducing this suffix using words that require no change in spelling to the base word (e.g., *asking*). **Note:** Words in shaded boxes are multisyllabic words that contain the highlighted ending.

-ing Words

acting	honking	sleeping	wishing
asking	jumping	smelling	yelling
bending	landing	speeding	contrasting
blinking	listing	spilling	contacting
brushing	looking	splashing	extending
calling	passing	stamping	harvesting
camping	planting	sticking	hollering
dressing	pressing	stitching	insisting
eating	pulling	telling	insulting
ending	quilting	trusting	inventing
falling	renting	turning	maintaining
farming	resting	twisting	publishing
filming	ringing	waiting	preventing
fishing	singing	walking	relaxing
helping	sinking	watching	requesting

-ing Phrases

farming and planting	looking before passing	resting and sleeping
honking a horn loudly	stitching and quilting	smelling the roses
walking on a bumpy path	acting on stage	brushing the dog's coat
harvesting the crops	publishing a book	extending the deadline
calling out loud	camping next weekend	splashing in the lake
helping with dinner	blinking its eyes	relaxing at home

-ing Sentences

The team is walking at the race next week.	We were walking and singing in the rain.
Brushing the dog's coat feels very relaxing.	Drivers should be looking before passing.
Resting and sleeping is good for your brain.	I was waiting to hear the ending of the story.
Farming and planting are not just done in the spring.	The dogs are jumping up to get food scraps off the table.
We meet every Thursday to do some stitching and quilting.	They said they will be harvesting the crops next week.
We lay back on the grass, watching the falling stars.	There was much yelling and hollering at the start of the race.
The large truck was speeding and honking its horn loudly.	Dad and Theo are planting flowers in the garden.

-s: plural noun; present-tense third-person singular verb

The suffix *-s* has two sounds: /s/ and /z/.

- When a base word ends with an unvoiced consonant (such as /k/, /p/, or /t/), the suffix *-s* is pronounced /s/.
- When a base word ends with a voiced consonant (such as /g/, /m/, /n/, or /ng/), the suffix *-s* is pronounced /z/.

It is used to form plural nouns, such as *cats* and *dogs*. It is also used to form present-tense, third-person, singular verbs, such as *runs* (*She runs*) and *plays* (*He plays*). **Note:** Words in shaded boxes are multisyllabic words that contain the highlighted ending.

-s Words (plural nouns)

-s Pronounced /s/			
bikes	cups	lights	ships
books	desks	lines	sticks
camps	forks	nuts	texts
carts	flutes	paths	trails
cats	gates	plants	treats
charts	hats	plates	trucks
cows	lakes	rocks	vases

The Ultimate Book of Phonics Word Lists for Grades 3–5 © by Laurie J. Cousseau and Rhonda Graff, Scholastic Inc.

athletes	insects	papers	secrets
baskets	letters	planets	students
comics	mistakes	robots	sunflowers
habits	pancakes	rockets	tulips

−s Pronounced /z/			
arms	farms	rugs	apples
birds	*flags	spoons	bananas
boys	games	*stains	beetles
bugs	germs	*stars	hotels
cars	girls	tails	margins
chairs	hills	trees	motels
clues	nerves	tubes	pebbles
coins	owls	twigs	reptiles
dogs	pens	wigs	robins
*dreams	ponds	yams	tables
*fans	quills	yards	windows

−s Words (present-tense, third-person, singular verbs)

−s Pronounced /s/			
asks	makes	taps	develops
hits	sits	thanks	prevents
hops	speaks	thinks	requests
jumps	starts	twists	unpacks

−s Pronounced /z/			
aims	makes	*shows	trims
brings	needs	slams	yells
calls	plays	*stands	combines
ends	rubs	swims	delivers
grabs	runs	tags	provides

*Words that are both nouns and verbs

The Ultimate Book of Phonics Word Lists for Grades 3–5 © by Laurie J. Cousseau and Rhonda Graff, Scholastic Inc.

-s Phrases

plates and forks	makes bikes	hops and jumps
plants and trees	speaks about books	insects on the plants
baskets of tulips	plates full of treats	unpacks the bag
hotels or motels	leaves on the trees	paper margins
twigs in the yard	dreams big	swims in a pool
boys on bikes	birds chasing bugs	hits a homerun
grabs the forks	many gates at the hotels	tulips and sunflowers
cats and dogs	tables and chairs	calls and yells
planets and stars	pens on the desks	robins resting on sticks

-s Sentences

The cats and dogs hid under the plants.	The dirt paths are full of pebbles.
The plants and trees are green in spring.	The lights are stars in the night sky.
Pack plates and forks for the picnic.	Fred makes bikes to ride on trails.
The reptiles rest on the rocks.	The boys and girls read comics.
The puppy hops and jumps to get its dish.	Her texts and letters end with a smile.
The paper had wide margins and lines.	There are many tables and chairs to set up.
He plays the banjo at shows in the summer.	The students use the margins on their papers.
The farmer calls and yells for the cows to come home.	The vases were filled with tulips and sunflowers.

TIP BOX

Some words, such as *bats, tags,* and *stamps,* can be used as plural nouns or singular, third-person verbs. These words can have multiple meanings.

The **bats** are in the cave.	The girl **bats** first in the lineup.
The **tags** on his shirts are itchy.	The player on first base **tags** the runner.
Put the **stamps** on the envelopes.	The toddler **stamps** her foot.

The Ultimate Book of Phonics Word Lists for Grades 3–5 © by Laurie J. Cousseau and Rhonda Graff, Scholastic Inc.

-es: plural noun; present-tense third-person singular verb

The suffix -es is pronounced /iz/. We use -es when the base word ends with -ss, -x, -sh, -ch, -z, or -tch. It is used to form plural nouns, such as *wishes* and *foxes*. It is also used to form third-person singular verbs, such as *misses* and *buzzes*.

-es Words

Plural Nouns			
boxes	*dresses	*latches	peaches
bushes	foxes	*lunches	pouches
churches	glasses	*matches	*taxes
classes	*hatches	*messes	*watches
*coaches	inches	*notches	*waxes
couches	*kisses	*patches	*wishes
Third-Person Singular Verbs			
buzzes	hisses	munches	smashes
cashes	hushes	passes	snatches
crunches	mashes	pushes	squishes
*dashes	misses	*sketches	*stitches
fetches	mixes	slouches	switches

*Words that are both nouns and verbs

-es Phrases

glasses to see sketches	dashes to the bushes	patches on the dresses
foxes in boxes	mashes and squishes	switches the sketches
hatches from an egg	messes up the table	peaches in pouches
dresses for school	snatches the toy	dashes for the finish line
cooking classes next week	misses by inches	making birthday wishes
waxes the cars and trucks	crunches on chips	counts the inches

-es Sentences

There were many foxes in boxes.	There were many patches on the dresses.
Shut the latches on all the boxes.	The glasses are full of fruit punch and ice.
The bee buzzes near the windows.	Pick some peaches for grandma's pie.
Henry kisses all his horses every morning.	The dresses are on the rack.
I needed my glasses to see all the sketches.	The twins made their birthday wishes and blew out the candles.
The snake hisses as it slithers on the grass.	He dashes to the bushes to win the contest.
She mashes and squishes the bananas to make cake.	She wishes for a few more inches to reach the top.
The artist switches the sketches at the show.	Kangaroos with pouches should not be on couches.

-er: comparing two / -est: comparing three or more

The suffixes -er and -est are of Anglo-Saxon origin. They are both comparative inflectional endings used with adjectives. The suffix -er is used to compare two things, while -est is used to compare three or more things. The suffix -er can also mean "person who" (see page 31).

-er, -est Words

-er	-est	-er	-est
brighter	brightest	higher	highest
cleaner	cleanest	kinder	kindest
cooler	coolest	longer	longest
faster	fastest	louder	loudest
fewer	fewest	lower	lowest
fresher	freshest	milder	mildest
greater	greatest	newer	newest
harder	hardest	prouder	proudest

The Ultimate Book of Phonics Word Lists for Grades 3–5 © by Laurie J. Cousseau and Rhonda Graff, Scholastic Inc.

-er cont.	-est cont.	-er cont.	-est cont.
quicker	quickest	straighter	straightest
sharper	sharpest	stricter	strictest
shorter	shortest	stronger	strongest
slower	slowest	sweeter	sweetest
smaller	smallest	warmer	warmest
smoother	smoothest	wilder	wildest
softer	softest	younger	youngest

-er, -est Phrases

stronger together	brighter star	smoother surface
smaller space	fewer in a bundle	sharper pencil point
slower turtle	can lower the price	warmer inside
milder weather	younger sister	shorter than my sister
lowest rung	freshest scent	mildest flavor
sweetest taste	smoothest velvet	kindest person
slowest car on the road	cleanest plate at the table	brightest light in the sky
freshest fruit in the bowl	greatest moment	loudest growl of the tigers

-er, -est Sentences

The brighter light helps us see more.	She is the fastest swimmer on the team.
We are stronger together than alone.	Abby has the longest braid I've seen.
At the lake, we bike at a slower pace.	I blended the soup, and it is now smoother.
The other runners on the track are faster.	The local market has the freshest fish.
To hear the sweetest sound, play the music louder.	That town has the cleanest streets and sidewalks.
My younger sister is the coolest person I know.	My dog has the loudest bark when greeting visitors.

Three Spelling Rules for Adding Suffixes

After students have practiced adding suffixes with no change to the base word (*small + er = smaller*), they can transition to working with words that require a change to the base word. There are three spelling generalizations to how a base word changes when a suffix is added: Drop *e*, Double the Final Consonant, and Change *y* to *i*.

Drop *e* when . . .

- the base word ends with an *e*.
- the suffix begins with a vowel.

Pattern: Drop the *e* on the base word when adding a suffix that starts with a vowel. If the suffix begins with a consonant, keep the *e*.

dance + er = dancer
face + ed = faced
hope + ing = hoping
like + able = likable
name + ed = named
time + ing = timing
wise + est = wisest

Double the Final Consonant when . . .

- the base word is one syllable.
- the base word has a single short vowel.
- the base word ends with a single consonant.
- the suffix begins with a vowel.

Pattern: If all the checkpoints are met, double the final consonant on the base word when adding a vowel suffix to protect the short vowel in the first syllable.

swim + ing = swimming
hop + ing = hopping
fan + ed = fanned
run + ing = running
plan + ed = planned
plot + ed = plotted
tap + ing = tapping
win + er = winner

Change *y* to *i* when . . .

- the base word ends with a *y*.
- the letter before the *y* is a consonant.

Pattern: Change the *y* to an *i* if the letter before the *y* is a consonant. If the letter before the *y* is a vowel, do not change the *y* to an *i*. The suffix can begin with a vowel or consonant . . .
EXCEPT when the suffix begins with an *i* (e.g., -*ing*, -*ish*).

beauty + ful = beautiful
carry + ed = carried
happy + ness = happiness
salty + er = saltier

joy + ful = joyful
cry + ing = crying

The Ultimate Book of Phonics Word Lists for Grades 3–5 © by Laurie J. Cousseau and Rhonda Graff. Scholastic Inc.

Suffix Spelling Rule #1: Drop *e*

The Drop *e* spelling rule is easiest to remember when approached with these two checkpoints:

Checkpoint 1: The base word ends with an *e*.

Checkpoint 2: The suffix begins with a vowel.

When both checkpoints are met, drop the *e* on the base word. If the base word ends with an *e* and the suffix begins with a consonant, do not drop the *e*. Just add the suffix.

Help students understand that the silent *e* is still attached to the base word even if it looks like it's no longer there. Although the term "drop the *e*" is frequently used, the *e* is not actually dropped. The *e* is "hiding" behind the newly placed suffix, still doing its job of making the vowel long. Keeping this in mind will make it easier for students to read these words correctly. For example, when we add *-ing* to the base word *hope*, it becomes *hoping* and not *hopping*.

It is good practice for students to build words by adding suffixes. Then they can work backward and isolate the base words and identify the suffixes. **Note:** Words in shaded boxes are multisyllabic words that contain the highlighted ending.

Drop *e* Words (Suffix begins with a vowel)

-ed			
change + ed = changed	note + ed = noted	trade + ed = traded	exclude + ed = excluded
chase + ed = chased	place + ed = placed	use + ed = used	excuse + ed = excused
close + ed = closed	save + ed = saved	vote + ed = voted	inflate + ed = inflated
dine + ed = dined	scrape + ed = scraped	wipe + ed = wiped	inhale + ed = inhaled
hike + ed = hiked	share + ed = shared	complete + ed = completed	invite + ed = invited
like + ed = liked	smile + ed = smiled	confuse + ed = confused	reduce + ed = reduced
mute + ed = muted	stripe + ed = striped	dislike + ed = disliked	surprise + ed = surprised
name + ed = named	swipe + ed = swiped	eliminate + ed = eliminated	update + ed = updated
-er			
bike + er = biker	drive + er = driver	ride + er = rider	trade + er = trader
brave + er = braver	fine + er = finer	safe + er = safer	time + er = timer
cute + er = cuter	hike + er = hiker	skate + er = skater	write + er = writer

-est			
brave + est = bravest	fine + est = finest	safe + est = safest	wide + est = widest
close + est = closest	huge + est = hugest	strange + est = strangest	white + est = whitest
cute + est = cutest	late + est = latest		

-ing			
bake + ing = baking	hide + ing = hiding	slope + ing = sloping	describe + ing = describing
bite + ing = biting	love + ing = loving	use + ing = using	escape + ing = escaping
blaze + ing = blazing	make + ing = making	wave + ing = waving	excuse + ing = excusing
come + ing = coming	quote + ing = quoting	adore + ing = adoring	invite + ing = inviting
dance + ing = dancing	rake + ing = raking	amaze + ing = amazing	inquire + ing = inquiring
date + ing = dating	rise + ing = rising	compete + ing = competing	participate + ing = participating
glide + ing = gliding	share + ing = sharing	compose + ing = composing	twinkle + ing = twinkling

-y			
grime + y = grimy	juice + y = juicy	noise + y = noisy	shine + y = shiny
ice + y = icy	lace + y = lacy	shade + y = shady	slime + y = slimy

Drop *e* Phrases

baking a pie	lacy fabric	saved me a seat
dancing wildly	making dessert	shady spot under the tree
hiding behind a curtain	noisy party	slimy worms
scraped the bowl	chased the cat	a skilled biker
a juicy pear in the bowl	the bravest of all	making time for fun
competing in a race	disliked the taste	inflated the balloon
participating in sports	an amazing friendship	invited to the party
twinkling stars at night	good writer	shared a link
voted today	wiped up the spill	updated the phone number

The Ultimate Book of Phonics Word Lists for Grades 3–5 © by Lewie J. Caravana and Rhonda Graff, Scholastic Inc.

Drop *e* Sentences

He was baking an apple pie for the picnic.	She saved me a seat at the concert.
We were dancing wildly at sunset.	The hedgehog was hiding in the woods.
The pink dress is made from lacy fabric.	I voted today and got a colorful sticker.
The noisy party lasted until dawn.	She is a skilled writer of children's books.
We hiked to the park, but it was closed.	The loving grandpa smiled at his adoring grandson.
We found a nice shady spot under an elm tree.	The slimy worms were used to catch many fish.
We are making dessert and sharing it with our friends.	We liked watching the twinkling stars last night.
She scraped the bowl until there was not a drop left.	The athletes are participating in the baseball contest.

Keep the *e* Words

When a base word ends in a silent *e* and the suffix begins with a consonant, keep the *e* when adding the suffix. **Note:** Words in shaded boxes are multisyllabic words that contain the highlighted ending.

careless	lonely	safety	completely
closely	lovely	shameless	excitement
cuteness	movement	stately	extremely
graceful	spiteful	strangely	management
grateful	namely	surely	measurement
hopeful	noiseless	timely	refinement
hopeless	peaceful	useful	rejoiceful
lateness	plateful	useless	resourceful
likely	rarely	wisely	revengeful
likeness	rudeness	writes	settlement
lively	safely	zones	sincerely

Suffix Spelling Rule #2:
Double the Final Consonant

The Double the Final Consonant spelling rule is easiest to remember when approached with these four checkpoints:

Checkpoint 1: The base word is one syllable.

Checkpoint 2: The base word has one short vowel.

Checkpoint 3: The base word ends with a single consonant.

Checkpoint 4: The suffix begins with a vowel.

Double the final consonant on the base word when all four checkpoints are met. By doubling the consonant, the short vowel in the base word is protected and remains short.

It is good practice for students to build words by adding suffixes. Then they can work backward and isolate the base words and identify the suffixes.

Double the Final Consonant Words

-ed			
clap + ed = clapped	grin + ed = grinned	mop + ed = mopped	snap + ed = snapped
drag + ed = dragged	grip + ed = gripped	plan + ed = planned	step + ed = stepped
drip + ed = dripped	hop + ed = hopped	rip + ed = ripped	stop + ed = stopped
fit + ed = fitted	hug + ed = hugged	skid + ed = skidded	tap + ed = tapped
flip + ed = flipped	hum + ed = hummed	skip + ed = skipped	trip + ed = tripped
grab + ed = grabbed	map + ed = mapped	shop + ed = shopped	wag + ed = wagged

-er			
bat + er = batter	flat + er = flatter	run + er = runner	swim + er = swimmer
drum + er = drummer	hot + er = hotter	sad + er = sadder	win + er = winner
fat + er = fatter	jog + er = jogger	spin + er = spinner	zip + er = zipper

-est			
big + est = biggest	fit + est = fittest	hot + est = hottest	sad + est = saddest
dim + est = dimmest	flat + est = flattest	mad + est = maddest	thin + est = thinnest

-ing			
chop + ing = chopping	grin + ing = grinning	ship + ing = shipping	step + ing = stepping
dig + ing = digging	pet + ing = petting	sip + ing = sipping	tap + ing = tapping
drip + ing = dripping	plan + ing = planning	sit + ing = sitting	tug + ing = tugging
flap + ing = flapping	quit + ing = quitting	spin + ing = spinning	win + ing = winning

The Ultimate Book of Phonics Word Lists for Grades 3–5 © by Laurie J. Cousseau and Rhonda Graff, Scholastic Inc.

–y			
fog + y = foggy	grit + y = gritty	mud + y = muddy	star + y = starry

Do NOT Double the Consonant if . . .

the base word ends with two consonants			
colder	lifted	quilting	trusting
fishing	missed	rested	wanted
grumpy	planted	sorted	wished
jumping	pressed	starting	yelled
the base word has two vowels			
coolest	painted	sailing	trained
grainy	reading	speaker	waiting
the suffix begins with a consonant			
cupful	gladness	shipment	spotless
dimly	maps	skips	stars
the base word ends with the letter x, which is never doubled			
boxing	fixed	foxes	taxes

Double the Final Consonant Phrases

biggest rabbit	hopped along	a stuck zipper on the coat
water dripping in the sink	swift runner	petting a puppy
foggy morning	spins a spinner	wagged her tail
gritty taste	stepping on stones	snapped a long twig
gripped the jar tightly	grinning proudly	spinning quickly
sipping a hot drink	muddy feet	starry night skies
hugged her little brother	planning a trip	mapped out the trip
grabbed a snack	tapped a tune	quitting too soon
grinning widely	strong swimmer	tugging a heavy rope

The Ultimate Book of Phonics Word Lists for Grades 3–5 © by Laurie J. Cousseau and Rhonda Graff, Scholastic Inc.

Double the Final Consonant Sentences

I saw the biggest rabbit in the grass.	After winning the race, we grinned widely.
She dripped water drops on the floor.	We hopped and skipped along the path.
It was a misty and foggy morning.	She is a swift runner and strong swimmer.
We grabbed a snack and headed home.	I tripped over a snapped twig on the path.
We gazed up at the starry night skies.	The bike skidded to a sudden stop.
They mopped up the spill quickly.	The talented drummer played a gig.
I had a gritty taste in my mouth.	We sat sipping a cold drink on a hot day.
Since it was a foggy morning, it was hard to see.	He grabbed a snack on the way to the game.
We snapped our fingers in time to the music.	She hugged her little brother when he started to cry.
We planned our trip and mapped out the way.	She is stepping across the stones in the river.

Suffix Spelling Rule #3: Change *y* to *i*

The Change *y* to *i* spelling rule is easiest to remember when approached with these two checkpoints:

Checkpoint 1: The base word ends with a *y*.

Checkpoint 2: The letter before the *y* is a consonant.

Change the *y* to an *i* when adding a suffix, whether it begins with a vowel or consonant, EXCEPT if the suffix begins with an *i* (e.g., *-ing* or *-ish*). Then, leave the *y* when adding the suffix.

It is good practice for students to build words by adding suffixes. Then they can work backward and isolate the base words and identify the suffixes. **Note:** Words in shaded boxes are multisyllabic words that contain the highlighted ending.

Change *y* to *i* Words

-ed			
cry + ed = cried	try + ed = tried	hurry + ed = hurried	study + ed = studied
dry + ed = dried	carry + ed = carried	marry + ed = married	tally + ed = tallied
fry + ed = fried	copy + ed = copied	reply + ed = replied	worry + ed = worried

The Ultimate Book of Phonics Word Lists for Grades 3–5 © by Laurie J. Cousseau and Rhonda Graff, Scholastic Inc.

-er / -est			
cute + est = cutest	cuddly + est = cuddliest	lovely + er = lovelier	shady + er = shadier
bumpy + er = bumpier	funny + er = funnier	lucky + est = luckiest	silly + er = sillier
cozy + est = coziest	happy + est = happiest	messy + er = messier	tiny + est = tiniest

-es			
fry + es = fries	bunny + es = bunnies	fairy + es = fairies	party + es = parties
sky + es = skies	city + es = cities	hobby + es = hobbies	penny + es = pennies
spy + es = spies	country + es = countries	lady + es = ladies	pony + es = ponies
baby + es = babies	factory + es = factories	lily + es = lilies	puppy + es = puppies

-ful			
beauty + ful = beautiful	bounty + ful = bountiful	fancy + ful = fanciful	plenty + ful = plentiful

-ness			
happy + ness = happiness	icy + ness = iciness	lazy + ness = laziness	lonely + ness = loneliness

Do NOT Change the y to i if . . .

the suffix begins with an i			
babyish	crying	hurrying	studying
copying	drying	spying	trying
there is a vowel before the y			
boys	enjoyment	payment	stayed
chimneys	journeys	playful	toys
decayed	joyous	pulleys	trays
delayed	keys	relayed	turkeys
displayed	monkeys	sprayed	valleys
donkeys	obeyed		

Change *y* to *i* Phrases

beautiful babies	replied to the request	many countries
studied hard for the exam	hurried home	starry skies
secret spies	played with the puppies	studied all night
cried out loud	carried her bookbag	cutest bunnies on the lawn
lilies in a tall vase	tiniest ponies in the field	distant cities
cuddliest bunnies	fanciful imagination	the silliest faces
funniest joke	french fries to eat	many pennies in a jar
rested in the coziest chair	rides the ponies	dried the clothes

Change *y* to *i* Sentences

The beautiful fairies were magical.	The lively ponies were in the stable.
Put the extra pennies in the jar.	We carried the packages in the house.
The secret spies hid in the tiniest space.	Hot french fries taste so good with salt.
I found the coziest chair to read in.	The ladies plan to visit many countries.
There were so many beautiful babies to hold.	I studied very hard for the test.
They carried the sweet puppies in a woven basket.	We had the bumpiest ride without a saddle.
Jerry told the funniest joke, and we all giggled.	We all sat under the starry skies and counted our blessings.
The cuddliest bunnies are hopping all over the garden.	Please place the lilies in a vase on the table.
We saw the tiniest ponies in the paddock at the farm.	We dried our wet clothes on the fence in the warm sun.

-er: person who

The suffix -er can be used to compare two things (see page 20) or to indicate a person who does something.

-er Words

archer	drummer	pitcher	skater
baker	farmer	player	swimmer
banker	firefighter	quitter	teacher
boater	fixer	reader	thinker
camper	gardener	researcher	waiter
catcher	golfer	rider	winner
climber	helper	runner	welder
dancer	jogger	seeker	worker
dreamer	painter	singer	writer

-er Phrases

the master baker	the modern dancer	the strong swimmer
the hiker and climber	the mystery writer	the researcher's helper
the expert welder's tools	the drummer's concert	the heroic firefighter
the abstract painter	the competing runner	a graceful skater
tipped the nice waiter	dairy farmer	organic gardener
seeker of truth	winning golfer	very hard worker

-er Sentences

The singer joined the band at the festival.	The jogger persisted up the hill.
The boater prefers a sailboat.	The farmer's rooster crowed at sunrise.
They will place their order with the waiter.	The golfer plays on sunny and rainy days.
The horse rider prefers to trot on the path.	The singer's beautiful voice won many hearts.
The master baker will cater the desserts for the wedding.	The older runner is swifter than the younger runner.

-er Sentences cont.	
The abstract painter created many works of modern art.	In the morning, the dairy farmer milks the cows.
The graceful skater spun and landed every jump.	The mystery writer provided a twist at the end of the story.
The organic gardener used natural fertilizer to grow the vegetables.	Many heroic firefighters received medals for their bravery.

-or: person who

The suffix *-or* is of Latin origin and is an unaccented ending pronounced /er/. It can mean a "person who," as in *actor* or *collector*. It is often used after the letter *t*. When *-or* is added to a base word, the word becomes a noun.

-or Words

actor	contractor	governor	professor
advisor	counselor	inspector	sailor
ancestor	creator	instructor	sculptor
author	decorator	inventor	senator
calculator	director	investigator	surveyor
collector	doctor	investor	survivor
conductor	donor	legislator	traitor
constructor	editor	narrator	visitor

-or Phrases

train conductor	a famous actor	biology professor
surfing instructor	interior decorator	a surprise visitor
ice sculptor	the school counselor	a helpful advisor
patient doctor	scientific calculator	creator of the game
generous donor	children's author	brave ancestors
collector of antique clocks	survivor of the storm	narrator of a story

-or Sentences

We had a surprise visitor in class today.	I want to go to school to become a doctor.
Who is your favorite children's author?	The counselor acted as a helpful advisor.
Where are your ancestors from?	The narrator tells a beautiful story of hope.
The ice sculptor created a beautiful swan for the display.	The actor works with the director to make a movie.
The history professor likes to take her class on field trips.	The inventor created a pen that never runs out of ink.
The donor gave warm food and clothing to families who needed help.	The inspector checked the house to be sure it was safe.

-ist: person who

The suffix -ist is of Latin origin and means "person who," as in artist and novelist. Words with the suffix -ist are nouns.

-ist Words

artist	dentist	naturalist	realist
balloonist	finalist	novelist	scientist
bicyclist	florist	optimist	soloist
biologist	flutist	organist	specialist
botanist	geologist	pessimist	tourist
cartoonist	guitarist	pharmacist	typist
chemist	impressionist	physicist	ventriloquist
columnist	journalist	pianist	violinist
cyclist	motorist	publicist	vocalist

-ist Phrases

dentist office	journalist's column	chemist's experiment
florist shop on the corner	impressionist style	novelist's notes
cyclist on the road	talented artist	finalist in the contest
marine biologist	scientist's research lab	such a pessimist
a true optimist	arranged by a florist	going to the dentist

-ist Sentences

Tina started working as a typist.	Drew studied to become a biologist.
The violinist's performance was incredible.	My friend is a talented artist and sculptor.
I read about that journalist last week in the newspaper.	Carla wants to become a chemist when she grows up.
I need to book an appointment with the dentist.	The coach of our soccer team is an optimist.
The publicist sent pictures of the artist's works to the museum.	George was fascinated with rocks, so he studied to become a geologist.
The artist enjoyed looking at the impressionist paintings.	The guitarist and violinist played while the vocalist sang.

-y: characterized by

The suffix -y is of Anglo-Saxon origin and used as a describing adjective. A nice way to introduce -y as a suffix is by referencing words related to weather, such as *rainy, sunny,* or *windy.*

-y Words

brawny	frosty	mighty	sleepy
bumpy	funny	misty	snowy
cheesy	gloomy	moody	soapy
chewy	grouchy	mossy	spicy
chilly	grumpy	oily	sticky
cloudy	hazy	pudgy	stormy
creamy	icy	rainy	sunny
crispy	itchy	risky	wavy
dirty	jolly	salty	wealthy
dreamy	juicy	sandy	whiny
dusty	jumpy	shiny	windy
foggy	lumpy	silly	yummy

-y Phrases

dusty trail	juicy orange	lumpy batter
icy roads after the storm	grouchy brother	sticky sap from the tree
sunny beach	itchy skin from a rash	mossy rock
cloudy day	a risky choice	windy day
chilly winter morning	shiny bracelets and rings	cheesy pizza
whiny toddler	soapy bubbles in the bath	moody teenager
spicy meal	crispy chips and dip	funny jokes
driving on a bumpy road	six silly puppies	wavy long hair
hazy skies	grumpy frown	oily gears
yummy ice cream	foggy morning	rainy season

-y Sentences

My dirty dog was jumpy.	The yummy pizza is crispy and cheesy.
The pancake batter felt lumpy and sticky.	I looked silly trying to eat a juicy orange.
The stormy skies cleared and made way for a sunny day.	The cowboy rode his horse down the dusty and bumpy trail.
It was windy at the beach, and my sandwich got sandy.	The mossy rocks become even more slippery in rainy weather.
I poured a glass of lemonade into a frosty, icy mug.	All the bug bites made me grumpy and itchy.
The meal was spicy, so I needed a frosty drink.	The crispy crackers taste so good with the creamy dip.
On hazy days, we can't see across the field.	The mossy rocks were wet and hard to walk on.
Her grumpy frown turned upside down when she smiled.	The oily gears on my bicycle left smears on my jeans.
The morning was so foggy, we could hardly see the mountains.	The six silly puppies became whiny when they wanted a yummy treat.

The Ultimate Book of Phonics Word Lists for Grades 3–5 © by Laurie J. Cousseau and Rhonda Graff, Scholastic Inc.

-ly: characteristic of

The suffix -ly is of Anglo-Saxon origin and is used as an adverbial ending that answers the question "how."

-ly Words

accidentally	finally	lovely	recently
annually	foolishly	monthly	sharply
anxiously	frequently	neatly	sincerely
badly	generally	necessarily	slightly
beautifully	gently	neighborly	slowly
bravely	gingerly	nicely	strangely
briefly	gladly	normally	strongly
carefully	gracefully	partially	suddenly
casually	happily	partly	sweetly
certainly	highly	perfectly	swiftly
closely	hopefully	practically	thankfully
correctly	hourly	promptly	unlikely
dangerously	lastly	proudly	usually
eagerly	lightly	quickly	weekly
easily	likely	quietly	widely
effortlessly	lively	rapidly	wrongly
eventually	lonely	really	

-ly Phrases

meet annually	widely known	folded the napkins neatly
nicely done	paddled swiftly on the lake	lightly salted
hourly wage	run away quickly	scared suddenly
quietly whispered	weekly shopping list	bravely set off
learned effortlessly	a lively group of kittens	arrived promptly
skipping happily	proudly displayed their art	a likely answer

The Ultimate Book of Phonics Word Lists for Grades 3–5 © by Laurie J. Cousseau and Rhonda Graff, Scholastic Inc.

-ly Sentences

I will gladly have another piece of cake.	Will likes his tea lightly sweetened.
The climber bravely reached the summit.	Mia petted the dog gently.
The weather today is partly cloudy.	The current flows swiftly downstream.
Eventually, the lonely horse quietly made a few friends.	The car drives quickly around the racetrack.
The camper woke up and made his bed neatly after being asked nicely.	It is widely known that the sun rises in the east.
The princess lived happily ever after in her castle on the hill.	The clothing was neatly folded in my backpack.
It was lovely to see the ballerina dance gracefully across the stage.	I heard a strange noise, so my heart beat rapidly.

-ment: result of an action; state of

The suffix -ment is of Anglo-Saxon origin and is often pronounced with a schwa, as in /mənt/. It means "the result of" or "state of an action." This meaning can be abstract for some students, so have them refer back to the base word. For example, achievement means "the result of achieving," and excitement is "the state of being excited." When the suffix -ment is added to a base word, the word becomes a noun.

-ment Words

accompaniment	basement	equipment	postponement
achievement	contentment	excitement	pronouncement
acknowledgement	development	government	refreshment
adjustment	disappointment	improvement	replacement
advancement	employment	judgment	requirement
ailment	encouragement	management	settlement
appointment	engagement	movement	shipment
argument	enjoyment	pavement	statement
assignment	entertainment	payment	treatment

-*ment* Phrases

huge achievement	a minor ailment	government agent
great excitement	opening statement	homework assignment
faulty equipment	complete contentment	huge disappointment
in the damp basement	an overnight shipment	provided encouragement
specific requirements	a dentist appointment	tasty refreshments
slight adjustment	smiled with contentment	quick movements
postponement due to weather	opportunities for advancement	needs a replacement battery

-*ment* Sentences

We recently moved into a basement apartment.	The dragon caused a lot of fear and excitement.
My parents made a payment for my new bike.	The refreshment was yummy on a hot day.
The document contained many truthful statements.	Rain and thunder caused the postponement of the match.
The shipment of books went missing, so we had to get replacements.	The sculptor uses many pigments and equipment to make art.
The team's big achievement caused much excitement!	I am running late for my appointment with the dentist.
At the party, they provided refreshments and entertainment	There are specific requirements for the math assignment
They made a slight adjustment to the daily schedule.	She smiled with contentment as she lay on the beach.
The opening statement to the speech was quite long.	It was a huge disappointment when we lost the soccer game.

-ness: state of

The suffix -ness is of Anglo-Saxon origin and means "the state of being." This meaning can be abstract for some students, so have them refer back to the base word. For example, *happiness* means "the state of being happy" or *silliness* means "the state of being silly."

-ness Words

bitterness	emptiness	illness	redness
business	fairness	kindness	rudeness
cheerfulness	fierceness	lateness	sharpness
cleverness	fitness	likeness	sickness
closeness	freshness	loneliness	soreness
dampness	fullness	loveliness	stillness
darkness	goodness	madness	thickness
dryness	greatness	nearness	weakness
eagerness	happiness	readiness	wildness

-ness Phrases

business class	soreness from exercise	laundered freshness
pure happiness	ankle weakness	stillness of the lake
fitness goals	redness from a rash	full of goodness
notable kindness	wild fierceness	in complete darkness
lots of cheerfulness	stillness in the night	dampness in the cellar
a pencil's sharpness	eagerness to begin	won't stand for rudeness

-ness Sentences

Our business has been open for a year.	I am working on my fitness goals.
The injury caused soreness in my leg.	The stillness of the lake looked like glass.
Your kindness is much appreciated.	Oh, my goodness, that peach was ripe.
Pure happiness is watching a beautiful sunset.	In my eagerness, I bumped my elbow on the fence.
After the power went out, we were left in darkness.	My biggest weakness is giving my dog treats even though she is on a diet.
The dampness of the basement made it smell moldy.	The freshness of the laundry smells like sweet lavender.

-ful: full of / -less: without

The suffixes -ful, which means "full of" and -less, which means "without," are of Anglo-Saxon origin. When -ful and -less are added to base words, the words become adjectives. Remind students that the suffix -ful has a single l, unlike the word full, which has two ls.

-ful, -less Words

-ful			
awful	flavorful	meaningful	skillful
bashful	forceful	mindful	sorrowful
beautiful	forgetful	mouthful	spoonful
bountiful	frightful	painful	spiteful
careful	graceful	peaceful	tactful
cheerful	grateful	playful	thankful
colorful	handful	powerful	thoughtful
delightful	harmful	respectful	useful
doubtful	helpful	restful	wasteful
dreadful	hopeful	roomful	watchful
fearful	joyful	shameful	wonderful

-less			
ageless	harmless	noiseless	sunless
blameless	hatless	painless	tasteless
bottomless	helpless	powerless	thoughtless
breathless	homeless	priceless	tactless
careless	hopeless	relentless	timeless
countless	joyless	restless	treeless
endless	lawless	shapeless	useless
faultless	meaningless	sleepless	voiceless
fearless	mindless	speechless	weightless
flawless	motionless	spotless	windless
friendless	nameless	starless	worthless

The Ultimate Book of Phonics Word Lists for Grades 3–5 © by Laurie L Crousseau and Rhonda Graff Scholastic Inc

-ful, -less Phrases

restful night's sleep	hopeful message	watchful eye
a colorful rainbow	graceful dancer	beautiful flower
grateful student	be careful	a delightful evening
cheerful baby	flavorful soup	peaceful state of mind
fearless leader	endless buffet	thoughtless actions
a priceless moment	a flawless performance	spotless bedroom
harmless flying insect	useless equipment	breathless after a run
starless skies	felt helpless	a timeless tale

-ful, -less Sentences

The surfers were grateful for the beautiful sunrise.	We spent a delightful evening listening to wonderful music.
Please be respectful of your wonderful classmates.	The weather center tracks the powerful storm with a watchful eye.
The graceful birds flew over the treeless fields.	The colorful rainbow left the hikers speechless.
Did you try a spoonful of pudding at the endless buffet?	It is helpful to save your useless scraps and make compost.
It is hopeless to think I will remember because I am so forgetful.	The fearless sailor faced the wind and powerful waves.
The fearless eagle sat motionless as it watched over its nest.	The children were restless and needed to move.

Opposite Words

When teaching the suffixes -ful and -less, you may want to introduce opposite words, such as colorful and colorless.

harmful	harmless		restful	restless
helpful	helpless		tactful	tactless
hopeful	hopeless		useful	useless

-en: made of; cause to be

The suffix -en is of Anglo-Saxon origin and is pronounced /ən/, as in wooden. Words that end with the suffix -en can be verbs, as in listen, or adjectives, as in golden. In words like golden, woolen, or wooden, the suffix -en can mean "made of." In words like brighten, sharpen, or strengthen, -en can mean "cause to be."

-en Words

brighten	forgotten	hidden	soften
broaden	frighten	lengthen	spoken
broken	frozen	loosen	strengthen
darken	given	molten	sweeten
deepen	glisten	oaken	thicken
fallen	golden	roughen	unbroken
fasten	handwritten	sharpen	weaken
flatten	harden	shorten	woolen
flaxen	heighten	silken	written

-en Phrases

a broken light bulb	fasten your seat belt	a written letter
frozen peas in a bag	woolen blanket	will sharpen the pencils
golden hour	molten lava	silken dress
will thicken the milkshake	can loosen the knot	sweeten with sugar
hidden camera	fallen leaves	brighten our day
will soften the butter	hidden pictures	soft spoken

-en Sentences

I sweeten my ice tea with sugar.	There is broken glass on the sidewalk.
She wrote her sister a handwritten note.	I haven't spoken to our new neighbor yet.
They planted golden tomatoes in their garden.	He used a power tool to loosen the screws.
Can we heighten the ceiling in the living room?	His grandmother wove him a woolen blanket for his birthday.
The sunlight glistened on the shimmering ocean waves.	You need to shorten those jeans by an inch, or they will drag on the ground.

The Ultimate Book of Phonics Word Lists for Grades 3–5 © by Laurie J. Cousseau and Rhonda Graff, Scholastic Inc.

-ar: pertaining to

The suffix -ar is of Latin origin and is another unaccented ending pronounced /er/.
It indicates an adjective or noun.

-ar Words

angular	grammar	nuclear	similar
beggar	granular	particular	solar
cellar	insular	polar	spectacular
circular	linear	rectangular	stellar
collar	lunar	regular	triangular
dollar	molecular	scholar	vinegar

-ar Phrases

lunar calendar	spectacular fireworks	linear path
solar eclipse	polar bear	apple cider vinegar
granular sand	stellar painting	dog collar
rectangular-shaped room	a grammar lesson	costs one dollar
smart scholar	regular piano lessons	similar in taste

-ar Sentences

The art display is colorful and spectacular.	The lemonade costs one dollar per glass.
The dog's collar is bright pink, so it is easy to spot.	You can store vegetables in the cool cellar.
The tortilla chips are triangular and perfect for dipping.	When baking soda and vinegar are mixed together, they make a messy foam.
We watched the spectacular fireworks from our backyard.	When I baked the cookies, the sugar was very granular.
Do you prefer pizza that is circular or rectangular?	The baker is very particular about the way he kneads the bread.
The regular programming was interrupted for a broadcast about the coming storm.	We missed our monthly visit to the zoo to see our favorite polar bear.

-able / -ible: able to

The suffixes -able and -ible are of Latin origin and pronounced with a schwa /əbl/. Both suffixes are adjective endings. They mean "able to," as in fixable ("able to be fixed") and audible ("able to be heard"). Although the spellings of these suffixes are often confused, -able is typically attached to a base word, such as fix or bend, while -ible is attached to a bound root (see page 87), such as aud or vis.

-able Words

acceptable	disposable	mixable	replaceable
affordable	drinkable	movable	respectable
agreeable	durable	noticeable	seasonable
applicable	enjoyable	passable	sociable
avoidable	fixable	payable	suitable
believable	flammable	peaceable	teachable
bendable	honorable	playable	thinkable
breakable	irritable	predictable	tolerable
charitable	laughable	preventable	trainable
comfortable	likable	probable	usable
controllable	lovable	questionable	valuable
dependable	manageable	reasonable	washable
despicable	memorable	regrettable	workable

-able Phrases

durable fabric	valuable treasure	comfortable couch
teachable moment	noticeable scar	playable clay
predictable ending	charitable donation	passable grade
a preventable accident	seasonable weather	enjoyable work
dependable friend	washable school glue	suitable for children
probable results	regrettable decision	memorable event
irritable baby	disposable cup in the trash	lovable puppy

The Ultimate Book of Phonics Word Lists for Grades 3–5 © by Laurie J. Cousseau and Rhonda Graff, Scholastic Inc.

-*able* Sentences

Now I'm in a much more agreeable mood.	The heavy desk is barely movable.
The rare card has become very valuable.	I slept in the comfortable bed all night.
The down winter jackets are washable.	The broken vase is replaceable.
The soccer net is quite durable, so it will last a long time.	The old truck is dependable and always makes it home.
It was a good story, but the ending was predictable.	We have only about three hours of usable daylight left.

-*ible* Words

accessible	divisible	impossible	plausible
admissible	edible	incredible	possible
audible	eligible	inflexible	reproducible
collapsible	fallible	invincible	responsible
collectible	flexible	irresistible	reversible
convertible	forcible	irresponsible	sensible
credible	gullible	legible	tangible
deductible	horrible	negligible	terrible
digestible	illegible	permissible	visible

-*ible* Phrases

edible candy hearts	collectible toys	sensible outfit
credible witness	impossible task	terrible view of the stage
responsible driver	possible choices	convertible car
a flexible gymnast	visible change in weather	irresistible panda cubs
legible handwriting	eligible to play sports	an incredible experience
collapsible basket	barely audible	felt invincible

-*ible* Sentences

The number 9 is divisible by 3.	We are flexible with our vacation plans.
The rotten peach tasted horrible.	The juicy red strawberry was irresistible.
Place the collapsible basket in the trunk.	What other possible option did you have?
Her quiet voice was barely audible in the crowd.	When it warmed up, the snow was no longer visible.
The cool shorts are reversible and can be purple or green.	Their terrible driveway is rocky and bumpy.

-*age:* place; condition of; pertaining to

The suffix -*age* is of Anglo-Saxon origin and can mean "place," as in *village* or *cottage*. It can also mean "pertaining to," as in *wreckage* or *yardage*. It is pronounced /əj/, with a schwa. It can be a noun, verb, or adjective.

-*age* Words

acreage	cottage	leverage	plumage
adage	courage	luggage	salvage
advantage	damage	manage	shortage
average	dosage	marriage	spoilage
baggage	frontage	message	storage
beverage	garbage	mileage	voyage
blockage	heritage	package	wreckage
cabbage	language	passage	yardage

-*age* Phrases

baggage claim	beverage cart	garbage truck
clear message	salvage yard	language lesson
average grades	luggage rack	storage unit
opens the package	traced her long heritage	a purple cabbage
a big piece of luggage	cleared the blockage	a refreshing beverage
takes great courage	a long and narrow passage	happy marriage

The Ultimate Book of Phonics Word Lists for Grades 3–5 © by Laurie J. Cousseau and Rhonda Graff. Scholastic Inc.

-age Sentences

I will carry my luggage up to my room.	What is the mileage on grandpa's old car?
We are vacationing at the cottage this summer.	We picked up our luggage at the baggage claim at the airport.
Ben needs to build up his courage to jump into the cold pool.	How do you manage to juggle six balls at the same time?
The garbage truck always arrives early Tuesday mornings.	What language class are you taking next year?
I'll send you a message when I get back home later tonight.	Due to bad weather, there is a shortage of oranges this year.

-ous: having; full of

The suffix *-ous*, pronounced /us/, is of Latin origin and can mean "full of," as in *famous*, or "having," as in *courageous*. It is used as an adjective.

-ous Words

boisterous	famous	mountainous	prosperous
courageous	frivolous	nervous	rigorous
dangerous	hazardous	numerous	scandalous
disastrous	humorous	outrageous	superfluous
enormous	jealous	perilous	tremendous
fabulous	joyous	poisonous	unanimous

-ous Phrases

unanimous decision	boisterous laughter	mountainous landscape
a poisonous snake	outrageous outfits	enormous hug
joyous celebration	jealous about nothing	a perilous journey
tremendous audition	famous actor	accepted numerous requests
humorous and playful banter	nervous about the performance	rigorous after-school schedule

-ous Sentences

This area of New England is mountainous.	His humorous jokes made us laugh.
Dean had a fabulous dance audition.	Her laughter is a joyous sound.
All work has to meet rigorous standards.	Delete the superfluous details.
Penny put in a tremendous amount of time on the project.	Take a long hike through the mountainous landscape.
This season, we grew the most enormous pumpkin in our patch.	When we go hiking, I am always on the lookout for poisonous snakes.
The circus has some famous performers and acrobats.	That was one of the most outrageous stunts I have ever seen.

-us: basic ending

Like the suffix -ous, the ending is pronounced /us/. It is commonly found at the end of a multisyllabic noun.

-us Words

abacus	circus	hippopotamus	papyrus
asparagus	crocus	lotus	radius
bonus	exodus	minus	rumpus
cactus	focus	nautilus	stimulus
census	fungus	octopus	tetanus
chorus	hibiscus	onus	virus

-us Phrases

flowering hibiscus	laser focus	nautilus shell
green asparagus	bright yellow fungus	octopus in the ocean
friendly hippopotamus	tetanus shot	a cactus in the dry desert
blooming lotus flower	singing in a chorus	talented circus performers
radius of a circle	ten minus five	eating asparagus and carrots

The Ultimate Book of Phonics Word Lists for Grades 3–5 © by Laurie J. Cousseau and Rhonda Graff Scholastic Inc.

-us Sentences

What is 20 minus 8?	Saffron comes from the crocus.
I saw a friendly octopus when I went scuba diving.	The weather channel reported that it's going to be minus four degrees tonight.
I would like to have a prickly cactus to put on my desk.	Let's grill asparagus and steak for dinner tonight.
The hippopotamus said, "Let the wild rumpus begin."	Did you know that the nautilus is related to the octopus?
Two nights a week, we have chorus rehearsal.	Please focus your attention to the center of the stage.

-ant: one who; that which

The suffix -ant is of Latin origin and pronounced /ənt/. It means a "person who," as in defendant. Students might confuse the suffix -ant with -ent (page 50) because they are pronounced the same but have different spellings. Explain that the suffix -ant may be used after a hard c or g, as in applicant or elegant. Reading widely can help reinforce these spellings for students. The suffix -ant can be a noun or adjective ending.

-ant Words

abundant	dominant	inhabitant	relevant
accountant	dormant	jubilant	reluctant
applicant	entrant	merchant	remnant
arrogant	fragrant	mutant	resonant
assistant	gallant	observant	stagnant
defendant	hesitant	occupant	tenant
defiant	ignorant	participant	tolerant
descendant	immigrant	pendant	triumphant
distant	important	pleasant	unpleasant

-*ant* Phrases

accountant firm	arrogant attitude	relevant message
gallant knight	fragrant perfume	dominant panther
unpleasant taste	stagnant water	virtual assistant
reluctant to compete	an organized assistant	a hesitant participant
pendant on a necklace	an important notice	jubilant after the victory
across distant mountains	many observant neighbors	a trustworthy applicant

-*ant* Sentences

The jubilant fans celebrated after the win.	I am hesitant to walk over the old bridge.
I don't know why she's always so unpleasant.	He can be very pleasant when he wants to be.
This fall, we had an abundant harvest from our garden.	In hot summer months, stagnant water can smell awful.
Anita enjoyed a pleasant afternoon sitting in her backyard.	The soccer team had a triumphant season and won the championship.
The salesperson came to the meeting with her assistant.	The observant crossing guard kept the children safe.

-*ent:* one who is or does

The suffix -*ent* is of Latin origin and pronounced /ənt/. The suffix -*ent* can mean "one who is," as in *president*. Students might confuse the suffix -*ent* with -*ant* (page 49) because they are pronounced the same but have different spellings. The suffix -*ent* may be used after a soft *c* or *g*, as in *innocent* or *intelligent*, or after *qu*, as in *frequent*. Reading widely can help reinforce these spellings for students. The suffix -*ent* can be a noun or adjective ending.

-*ent* Words

absorbent	client	current	different
accident	competent	dependent	evident
adolescent	confident	despondent	excellent
affluent	consistent	detergent	frequent

-ent Words cont.			
imminent	innocent	negligent	persistent
incident	intelligent	opponent	president
ingredient	magnificent	permanent	recipient

-ent Phrases

persistent morning rain	intelligent students	consistent attention
make a permanent move	a small accident	liquid detergent in a bottle
innocent choice	absorbent towels	local ingredient
a confident adolescent	an imminent storm	frequent visitors
had to report the incident	a different story to read	a worthy opponent
election for class president	current weather forecast	magnificent sunrise
recipient of the award	grew despondent	an excellent meal

-ent Sentences

An imminent storm is brewing in the west.	Miranda is running for class president.
There's a magnificent view from the mountaintop!	Did you remember to buy detergent at the store?
Do you have every ingredient you need to make dinner?	I have my own style and don't keep up with the current trends.
You must stay consistent if you want to create a lasting habit.	To make intelligent decisions, we must be fully informed.
We adopted the stray dog we found on the street and gave her a permanent home.	These paper towels are much more absorbent than those napkins.
The recipient of the award stood on the stage holding her medal.	Read the newspaper every day to be aware of current events.
The owl in our backyard seems to be a permanent fixture this winter.	Dad and I cooked an excellent meal last night.

The Ultimate Book of Phonics Word Lists for Grades 3–5 © by Laurie J. Cousseau and Rhonda Graff, Scholastic Inc.

-al: pertaining to

The suffix -al is of Latin origin and is pronounced /əl/, like the suffix -el (page 53). This sound might be confused with the Anglo-Saxon final stable syllable consonant + le. Consonant + le words are often basic vocabulary words, such as bubble and maple. The suffix -al often indicates an adjective, as in legal.

-al Words

annual	final	mythical	reversal
arrival	formal	natural	scandal
betrayal	general	neutral	signal
central	glacial	nominal	skeletal
choral	global	numeral	social
coastal	gradual	optional	societal
comical	immortal	oral	special
continental	interval	original	spiral
crystal	legal	oval	survival
cynical	literal	partial	tidal
decimal	lyrical	paternal	tribal
dental	maternal	pedal	trivial
diagonal	mental	pedestal	tutorial
digital	mineral	personal	typical
ethical	minimal	racial	verbal
facial	moral	refusal	virtual
factual	mortal	removal	vocal
fictional	musical	rental	withdrawal

-al Phrases

formal attire	Oval Office	natural talent
continental breakfast	crystal ball	playing musical instruments
fictional character	dental exam	general rules
coastal waters	spiral-bound notebook	studying the skeletal system

The Ultimate Book of Phonics Word Lists for Grades 3–5 © by Laurie J. Cousseau and Rhonda Graff, Scholastic Inc.

-al Phrases cont.		
survival of the fittest	original ideas	drank mineral water
rusty bicycle pedals	perched on a pedestal	withdrawal from the account

-al Sentences

The animal's chances of survival were high.	Dom is trained as a dental nurse.
The lion statue was perched on a pedestal.	I made a withdrawal from the account.
The coastal river has many tidal waters.	There are dangerous tidal currents.
You can't use this phone for personal calls.	The Oval Office is in the White House.
The clean crystal waters of the lake were shining.	I think we'd better go back to our original plan.
The annual arrival of the geese signals migration in the fall.	Rudy oiled the rusty bicycle pedals before the race.
The hotel served a continental breakfast of muffins and orange juice.	The fictional characters had magical powers that transformed their world.

-el: indicating small size

The suffix -el is of Latin origin and is pronounced /əl/ (like the suffix -al, page 52). This sound might be confused with the Anglo-Saxon final stable syllable consonant + le. Consonant + le words are often basic vocabulary words, such as bubble and maple. The suffix -el commonly indicates a noun, as in novel.

-el Words

angel	fuel	motel	rebel
barrel	gravel	mussel	sequel
bushel	hotel	nickel	shovel
cancel	hovel	novel	towel
channel	jewel	panel	travel
dispel	kennel	parcel	tunnel
dowel	label	parcel	vessel
easel	marvel	pastel	vowel
enamel	model	pretzel	weasel

-el Phrases

bushel of blueberries	label maker	sparkling jewels
visited a dog kennel	may cancel plans	fluffy towel
teeth enamel	painting on the art easel	travel plans
model airplane	fictional novel	sang like an angel
barrel of ripe apples	gravel on the driveway	weasel in the garden
fuel for the engine	salted and twisted pretzel	delivered the parcel
will gather mussel shells	propel forward	pastel colors
motel off the highway	snow shovel	one hundred channels
short vowels	inside a dark tunnel	movie sequel

-el Sentences

The suspenseful novel is entirely fictional.	The barrel on the dock is full of fuel.
The pretzel is all natural and gluten free.	She sang like an angel on stage.
It was hard to see in the dark tunnel.	Flora dried off with a fluffy towel.
The special parcel contains many sparkling jewels.	Where would you like to travel this summer?
We collected mussel shells on the beach.	The fuel for the tractor engine is diesel.
Put wood glue on the dowels before hanging them on the wall.	The four middle syllables have the same vowel.
The watercolor painting is drying on the easel.	Our travel plans were interrupted by stormy weather.
The sequel was more exciting than the first movie.	We picked a bushel of blueberries to make jam.
He had to cancel his visit to his grandmother.	Wanda, the weasel, lives in the coastal forest.

The Ultimate Book of Phonics Word Lists for Grades 3–5 © by Laurie J. Cousseau and Rhonda Graff, Scholastic Inc.

-ic / -ical: pertaining to

The suffixes -ic and -ical are forms of the same suffix and are of Latin origin. The suffix -ic means "pertaining to," as in atmospheric. It commonly indicates an adjective, as in fantastic, but it can also be a noun, as in comic. The suffix -ical is actually a combination of two suffixes (-ic + -al) and also means "pertaining to," as in logical.

The spelling generalization -ic at the end of a multisyllabic word can be contrasted with -ck, which is commonly found after a short vowel at the end of one syllable word. Examples of -ck words include pack and stuck.

-ic, -ical Words

-ic			
acidic	comic	historic	plastic
acrylic	cosmetic	magic	poetic
allergic	critic	majestic	pragmatic
alphabetic	domestic	mechanic	public
arctic	drastic	metallic	realistic
artistic	electric	metric	republic
atmospheric	fantastic	mimic	rustic
basic	frantic	music	scholastic
chronic	garlic	optic	static
civic	gigantic	organic	topic
classic	graphic	pathetic	traffic
clinic	hectic	phonetic	tragic

-ical			
botanical	economical	illogical	political
chemical	electrical	logical	practical
chronological	ethical	magical	radical
classical	fantastical	medical	spherical
clerical	geographical	methodical	symmetrical
comical	grammatical	musical	technical
conical	historical	nautical	theatrical
critical	hysterical	periodical	tropical
diabolical	identical	physical	whimsical

The Ultimate Book of Phonics Word Lists for Grades 3–5 © by Laurie J. Cousseau and Rhonda Graff, Scholastic Inc.

-ic, -ical Phrases

focused on the topic	adding garlic and salt	a static character
plastic packaging	allergic reaction	classic rock music
rustic cabin	arctic ice	pragmatic solution
organic produce	helicopter mechanic	hectic morning
learning the basic facts	attending a baseball clinic	learning magic tricks
comical film	critical thinker	identical twins
conical shape	hysterical laughter	periodical check-ins
technical manual	electrical outlets	physical training and exercise
whimsical whirligigs	impending tropical storm	radical out-of-the-box ideas

-ic, -ical Sentences

The lemonade tastes way too acidic without sugar.	The rustic cabin next to Walden Pond is very famous.
Roland got stuck in traffic on his way to the rustic cabin.	The music sounds majestic in the historic theater.
The theatrical performance contains classic rock music.	Traffic cones and party hats are both conical in shape.
Radical, out-of-the-box ideas may result in important inventions.	The students have periodical check-ins with their instructor.
They were stranded on a tropical island and ate coconuts.	The journey through the tropical forest requires physical strength.
The periodical contains many political articles.	The identical twins are hysterical when they get together.
The movie was so comical it made me cry with laughter.	She stored the chemicals in chronological order according to when they expire.
The electrical engineer was hired to find the critical issue in the system.	The spherical metallic object turned out to be magical.
The whimsical whirligigs were placed in the front yard.	The impending tropical storm landed at nightfall.

The Ultimate Book of Phonics Word Lists for Grades 3–5 © by Laurie J. Cousseau and Rhonda Graff, Scholastic Inc.

-ture: pertaining to

The suffix -ture is of Latin origin and is pronounced /cher/. It means "pertaining to," as in departure. Linguistically, the -ure is attached to a root word ending in t, as in vent (adventure) or fact (manufacture), but it is easiest to teach -ture as one "chunk." The suffix -ture can indicate a noun or verb.

-ture Words

adventure	feature	manufacture	premature
agriculture	fixture	mature	puncture
architecture	fracture	miniature	rapture
capture	furniture	mixture	sculpture
conjecture	future	moisture	signature
creature	gesture	nature	stature
culture	horticulture	nurture	structure
curvature	juncture	overture	temperature
denture	lecture	pasture	texture
departure	legislature	picture	venture
expenditure	literature	posture	vulture

-ture Phrases

adventure awaits	literature course	bumpy texture
miniature horse	antique sculpture	concrete mixture
extreme temperature	painted picture	historic culture
grassy pasture	musical overture	creature in the field
departure from the plan	moisture in my eyes	extended a kind gesture
large-winged vulture	puncture in the flat tire	organize living room furniture
upright posture	light fixture	healed fracture
feature film	modern architecture	marble structure

-*ture* Sentences

Nate took careful notes during the teacher's lecture.	The large-winged vulture flew over the trees.
Use a fork to combine the sugar and butter until the mixture is light and fluffy.	Together, Jack and Jill went on a grand adventure.
Annie's departure time changed moments before boarding the flight.	That light fixture in your living room is beautiful.
They manufacture baskets made from recycled plastic.	During the summer, I like to enjoy nature by hiking local trails.
My teacher shares great literature with our class.	What career would you like to pursue in your future?
Our culture is represented by the recipes passed down to us through our ancestors.	The miniature horse stood alone in the field.

-*tion* / -*sion:* state of

The suffixes -*tion* and -*sion* are of Latin origin and are pronounced /shən/, like the suffix -*cian* (page 62). Both suffixes mean "state of." When these suffixes are attached to a root, the word becomes a noun. There are some generalizations to help with spelling choices. For younger students, it is easiest to teach -*tion* as one sound "chunk." However, as students get older, they can gain a new understanding of this suffix. Linguistically, a root ending with *t* is joined to the suffix -*on* by the letter *i*. The *i* is considered a connecting letter. For example, in the word *attraction*, the *i* connects the root *tract* to the suffix -*on*. You can say that the suffix shares the *t* with the root. The suffix -*sion* can also be pronounced /zhun/ in a word with one *s*, as in *version*. It is often attached to a root that ends in *s* or *ss*, as in *mission*.

-*tion* Words

action	attraction	connection	diction
adaptation	audition	construction	digestion
addition	caption	contention	direction
adoption	caution	contraption	division
affection	collection	correction	donation
ambition	commotion	creation	edition
animation	completion	decoration	elation
attention	condition	deduction	election

The Ultimate Book of Phonics Word Lists for Grades 3–5 © by Laurie J. Cousseau and Rhonda Graff, Scholastic Inc.

-tion Words cont.			
emotion	graduation	multiplication	quotation
equation	hesitation	nation	ration
eruption	hibernation	notion	reaction
exception	ignition	nutrition	reflection
exhaustion	infection	operation	relaxation
exhibition	injection	option	section
expiration	instruction	participation	solution
exploration	invitation	pollution	station
fiction	location	portion	subtraction
fraction	lotion	position	tradition
friction	mention	promotion	vacation
function	motion	question	variation

-tion Phrases

cleaned up the pollution	fire station	united nation
large portion of pie	hand lotion	undivided attention
work of fiction	children's section	volcanic eruption
holiday decoration	winter hibernation	loud commotion
asked for directions	addition and subtraction	handed out rations
offered a promotion	collection of contraptions	the perfect conditions

-tion Sentences

Place the decoration on the back door.	We plan to take a vacation next summer.
There was a mirrored reflection in the lake.	The construction crew is working on the bridge for the next three weeks.
The entire class received an invitation to the graduation party.	The students paid attention when the teacher introduced multiplication.
We love to visit the children's section of the library for story hour.	Did you know you can see your reflection in the shallow part of the lake?

The Ultimate Book of Phonics Word Lists for Grades 3–5 © by Laurie J. Cousseau and Rhonda Graff, Scholastic Inc.

-tion Sentences cont.	
The teacher gave clear directions for the project.	I intended to eat just a portion of pie, but then ate the whole thing!
What is all the commotion we can hear outside near the railway station?	I used my keen powers of deduction to solve the complicated subtraction problem.
Addition and subtraction have an opposite relationship.	We went on our canoe and joined the group to clean up river pollution.
The winter hibernation of bats takes place in caves.	The conditions were perfect for skiing after the snowstorm.
Carla's collection of contraptions is displayed in the science museum.	Bella ate an enormous portion of the blueberry pie and turned purple.
For the next two weeks, the section of the street next to the train station is getting paved.	Each section of the work of fiction is written from a different character's point of view.

-sion Words

admission	dimension	impression	procession
aversion	discussion	intermission	profession
collision	diversion	invasion	progression
compassion	division	mansion	propulsion
compression	envision	mission	provision
concession	erosion	occasion	revision
conclusion	evasion	omission	session
concussion	expansion	oppression	submission
confession	explosion	passion	supervision
confusion	expression	percussion	suspension
conversion	extension	permission	television
decision	fusion	persuasion	tension
delusion	illusion	possession	version
depression	immersion	precision	vision

The Ultimate Book of Phonics Word Lists for Grades 3–5 © by Laurie J. Cousseau and Rhonda Graff, Scholastic Inc.

-*sion* Phrases

kind expression	percussion instruments	another version
secret mission	magical illusion	clear vision
needed an extension cord	pack provisions	adult supervision
heard a loud explosion	saw a collision	developed a true passion
preventing soil erosion	fusion of musical styles	long discussion
division problem	speedy conclusion	in three dimensions
mounted the television on the wall	got popcorn at intermission	received permission for the trip

-*sion* Sentences

We visited the haunted mansion on the guided tour.	Her kind expression eased the tension in the room.
After a long discussion, we made revisions to the plan.	Once a week, they watched their favorite program on television.
The head guide provided provisions for our camping trip.	The local contractor proposed a new plan for expansion.
We received permission to go on a secret mission without supervision.	We need permission to ride our bikes to the store.
There was some confusion before she made her decision to join the expedition.	My impression of the magical illusion was a colorful explosion of glitter.
I made many revisions to the report to make it clearer.	During the intermission, we had a discussion about the first half of the play.
My view of the bicycle collision during the race was blocked by spectators.	Percussion can be the fusion of many musical styles.
I appreciate your kind expression when I asked for permission to take a break.	The procession wound its way through the village streets during the festival.
We can help prevent soil erosion by planting trees.	The artist developed a true passion for multidimensional sculpture.
The doctor treats her patients with compassion and understanding.	The omission of one digit resulted in the incorrect answer to the division problem.

-cian: person who

Like the suffixes -tion and -sion (page 58), the suffix -cian is of Latin origin and pronounced /shən/. It means "person who." When this suffix is attached to a root, the word becomes a noun. In the suffix -cian, the -an is often attached to a base word or root ending with -ic, as in magician. The i is a connecting letter, joining the root and the suffix. You can say that the suffix -cian shares the c with the base word. Knowing that the suffix -an means "person who," as in musician, helps students make correct spelling choices.

-cian Words

beautician	logician	optician	statistician
clinician	magician	pediatrician	tactician
dietician	mathematician	physician	technician
electrician	musician	politician	

-cian Phrases

talented musician	traveling magician	computer technician
skillful electrician	the child's pediatrician	the boat's tactician

-cian Sentences

An electrician came yesterday to fix the faulty wiring.	The child's pediatrician recommended rest and clear liquids.
The talented musician performs with the traveling magician.	The politician campaigned and delivered many speeches.
The school hired a computer technician to install the Wi-Fi.	Dan visited the dietician to discuss healthy eating habits.
When we steered off course, we were thankful for the boat's technician.	The optician did an eye examination and prescribed a new pair of glasses.

Mixed -tion, -sion, -cian Sentences

There was an exhibition of percussion instruments at the museum.	A mathematician is skilled with addition, subtraction, division, and fractions.
The main characters in the fictional account were magicians.	The electricians made a decision to make a donation to the fire department.

The Ultimate Book of Phonics Word Lists for Grades 3–5 © by Laurie J. Cousseau and Rhonda Graff, Scholastic Inc.

Mixed -tion, -sion, -cian Sentences cont.	
The students received permission to attend the event at the nation's capital.	The instructions included a list of provisions for the upcoming exploration.
The loud commotion outside the window was a clever diversion.	A portion of the proceeds were used to fund the expansion of the library.
The band members received an invitation to join the procession.	The revisions to the work of fiction included many corrections.

ti = /sh/ as in *-tial, -tient, -tious*
ci = /sh/ as *-cial, -cient, -cious*

The letters *-ti* and *-ci* can be considered Latin connectives because they attach to other suffixes, such as *-al*, *-ent*, and *-ous*. Since they are both pronounced /sh/, knowing them is very helpful for decoding. The Latin connective *-ti* is often used when the base word or root ends with a *t*, as in *presidential*. In words with *-ci*, the base word may have a *c*, as in *face/facial* or *artifice/artificial*. Multiple exposures to these types of words through reading and spelling will help students know which spelling pattern to use.

-ti, -ci Words

-tial			
celestial	credential	potential	spatial
circumstantial	essential	preferential	substantial
confidential	influential	presidential	torrential
consequential	initial	sequential	
-tient			
impatient	patient	quotient	sentient
-tious			
ambitious	fictitious	nutritious	scrumptious
cautious	flirtatious	ostentatious	superstitious
facetious	infectious	pretentious	
-cial			
artificial	crucial	judicial	social
beneficial	financial	official	special
commercial	glacial	provincial	

-cient			
ancient	efficient	proficient	sufficient
deficient	omniscient		
-cious			
atrocious	conscious	gracious	precious
auspicious	delicious	inauspicious	precocious
capricious	ferocious	malicious	spacious

-ti, -ci Phrases

confidential documents	cautious driver	social engagement
scrumptious meal	impatient children	presidential election
spacious van	commercial building	special tickets
torrential downpour	using sequential order	having a nutritious lunch
has great potential	after the initial meeting	fictitious characters
found ancient artifacts	cooked a delicious meal	learned a beneficial lesson
the ferocious lion's roar	a proficient student	no artificial ingredients

-ti, -ci Sentences

You are an essential part of the team.	I can help you set up a social media account.
They give out special awards to the winners.	We should make an efficient plan before the big event.
Tim was cautious while driving during the rainstorm.	Exercising weekly is beneficial for your overall health.
Our spacious kitchen can fit our extended family during the holidays.	They ate the delicious oranges during halftime to rehydrate for the game.
My dogs get impatient when they realize we are on our way to the dog park.	The local museum added the ancient rug to their collection.
After the initial meeting, we discussed the potential options.	The torrential rainfall caused substantial damage to the crops.
The fictitious characters became real to me as I got lost in the plot of the novel.	The study of ancient artifacts is beneficial to humankind.

Prefixes

Prefixes are morphemes that are attached to the beginning of a base word or root and change the meaning of the word. *Pre-* means "before," and *fix* means "to attach." There are many prefixes that are decodable based on their syllable structure. For example, the prefixes *pre-, de-, re-,* and *pro-* are open syllables with a long-vowel sound. The prefixes *un-, dis-, non-,* and *mis-* are closed syllables with a short-vowel sound. This allows some students easy access to longer words.

Prefixes are denoted with a dash afterwards, as in *un-*, to indicate that it is attached to the beginning of the word. Prefixes are also a common way to form antonyms (words with opposite meanings). For example: *happy/unhappy, allow/disallow, visible/invisible,* and *toxic/nontoxic*.

Both prefixes and suffixes are called "affixes" (*af-* meaning "to"). It is useful to teach students that when dealing with morphologically constructed words, a prefix may be pronounced with a schwa due to the accent falling on the root word; for example, *define* or *recite*.

Once students have a bank of prefixes and suffixes, word building is easy. Using the matrix below, for example, they can form words such as *reform, unformed, uniformly,* and *preform*.

Prefix	Root	Suffix
re-		*-ed*
un-		*-s*
uni-	*form*	*-ly*
pre-		*-ing*

Possible words			
reform	unform	uniform	preform
reformed	unformed	uniformed	preformed
reforms	unforms	uniforms	preforms
reforming	unforming	uniformly	preforming

un-: not

The prefix *un-* is of Latin origin and means "not." It can also indicate "opposite of," as in *happy* versus *unhappy*. It is an easy prefix to introduce early because it is decodable as a closed syllable.

un- Words

unable	uncut	unhappy	unplug
unaffected	undamaged	unharmed	unread
unafraid	undecided	unhealthy	unreal
unaltered	undo	unhurt	unreasonable
unanswered	undress	unimportant	unrest
unattractive	unearned	uninhabited	unruly
unavoidable	unearth	uninvited	unsafe
unaware	uneasy	unkind	unstable
unbelievable	unequal	unknown	unsteady
unbending	uneven	unlace	unsure
unbroken	uneventful	unlikely	unsympathetic
uncanny	unexpected	unlit	untangle
uncertain	unfair	unlock	unthinkable
unchanged	unfamiliar	unloved	untie
unclean	unfasten	unlucky	untold
unclear	unfinished	unmade	unusual
uncomfortable	unfit	unmistakable	unwanted
uncommon	unfold	unmoved	unwelcome
unconditional	unforgettable	unnatural	unwell
unconscious	unfortunate	unpack	unwind
uncontrollable	unfriendly	unpaid	unwise
uncover	ungrateful	unpleasant	unzip

The Ultimate Book of Phonics Word Lists for Grades 3–5 © by Laurie J. Cousseau and Rhonda Graff, Scholastic Inc.

un- Phrases

uncover clues	an unreal tale	unwise decision
unaffected area	unreasonable rules	unforgettable experience
uncommon path	unknown ending	unfinished homework
will unlace the sneakers	untold story	ungrateful response
unpaid bills	unclean kitchen table	unfair expectations
unpacked backpack	unfolded laundry on the bed	unfastened seat belt

un- Sentences

The unfinished board game sat on the table.	I am unable to attend the event tomorrow.
Please deal with the unfolded laundry on the bed.	He needed to unfasten his seat belt to get out of the car.
The friends shared the unforgettable experience of hiking the unknown trail.	He needed to uncover the boat so he could take it out in the morning.
Our basement flooded, but most of our belongings were unaffected.	The untold story was discovered in a secret journal.
The unfamiliar novel took an unexpected turn, which made it exciting to read.	The hard chair was uncomfortable to sit on and unsafe with only three legs.
The unzipped backpack should be unpacked because it is wet.	The unavoidable road closings made our drive an hour longer.
The unknown ending of the story kept us reading to find out what happened.	The caves are uninhabited, but people once lived in them long ago.
The camping trip in the mountains was an unforgettable experience.	We were unaffected by the travel changes, so we still arrived on time.
The detectives uncovered clues that revealed the untold story of the missing guest.	We took the uncommon path and discovered new adventures along the way.

The Ultimate Book of Phonics Word Lists for Grades 3–5 © by Laurie J. Cousseau and Rhonda Graff, Scholastic Inc.

in-: not; in

The prefix *in-* is of Latin origin and means "not," as in the word *inflexible*. It can also indicate "opposite of," as in *visible* versus *invisible*. It can also mean "in," as in the word *inside*.

The prefix *in-* is easy to introduce early because it is decodable as a closed syllable.

in- Words

in- (not or opposite of)			
inability	incomplete	indescribable	informal
inaccurate	inconclusive	indestructible	inhospitable
inactive	inconvenient	indirect	inhuman
inadequate	incorrect	indistinct	insane
inadvertent	incredible	indomitable	insecure
inappropriate	incredulous	inefficient	inseparable
inartistic	incurable	inevitable	invaluable
incapable	indefinite	inexact	invincible
incognito	indelible	infinite	invisible
incompetent	independent	inflexible	involuntary
in- (in)			
inbound	induct	inhabit	inside
include	infect	inhale	instill
income	inflate	inject	integrate
increase	influx	inlay	interior
incubate	inform	inner	intern
indent	infuse	input	invade
indoor	ingrown	inscribe	involve

The Ultimate Book of Phonics Word Lists for Grades 3–5 © by Laurie J. Cousseau and Rhonda Graff, Scholastic Inc.

in- Phrases

warm inside	high income	increase hours
inhabited campsite	inbound train	include others
incredible joy	indented sentence	inflated balloon
inactive status	invincible spirit	inconvenient location
incorrect answer	independent person	invisible superhero
incapable of answering	an inhospitable welcome	incredulous at the beauty
inhale deeply	a large indoor space	inevitable conclusion
inaccurate amount	indistinct shape	invaluable information
indefinite amount of time	inexact proportions	incubate the eggs

in- Sentences

She informed us of the changes.	Go inside if it starts to rain.
What is inside the secret treasure box?	Can we inscribe a plaque for the coach?
The first sentence of a paragraph should be indented.	The inbound train is on its way to the station.
Howard used inhuman strength when he lifted that heavy box.	Please don't forget to include your cousins on the guest list.
I am inflexible compared to my dance class partner.	We need to inflate all of these helium balloons.
The independent woman wanted to build her own cabin.	The explorers showed invincible spirit by reaching the peak of the mountain.
The invisible superhero saved the day, but no one saw him.	The incubated chicks hatched this morning.
We were incredulous at the beauty of the setting sun lighting up the horizon.	We received invaluable information about our whale research.
The indoor spaces of the museum were perfect for the art show.	They told her she has to wait an indefinite amount of time for the results.

non-: not

The prefix *non-* is of Latin origin and means "not." It can also indicate "opposite of," as in *fiction* versus *nonfiction*. It is an easy prefix to introduce early because it is decodable as a closed syllable.

non- Words

nonabsorbent	nonconsecutive	nonfactual	nonrealistic
nonacceptance	noncontagious	nonfat	nonremovable
nonactive	noncritical	nonfiction	nonresident
nonadjustable	noncurrent	noninfected	nonresponsive
nonathletic	nondairy	nonliving	nonsense
nonbeing	nondeductible	nonmember	nonstick
nonbeliever	nondescript	nonpartisan	nonstop
noncentral	noneffective	nonpayment	nontaxable
nonchalant	nonequivalent	nonproductive	nontoxic
noncommittal	nonexistent	nonprofit	nonuser
noncompliant	nonexplainable	nonqualified	nonverbal

non- Phrases

nonfat frozen treat	nonstop flight	reading nonfiction in class
nonprofit organization	wearing nondescript clothing	nonexistent material
nonstop fun	nonremovable sticker	nontaxable goods
nontoxic container	nonverbal sign	nondairy almond milk
nonresident of the state	nonpartisan government bill	nonrealistic story
absolute nonsense	nonproductive conversation	nonprofit food pantry
nonadjustable straps	nonconsecutive numbers	nonfactual reporting
skeptical nonbeliever	nonabsorbent towels	nonstick pan
noncentral location	nonmember of the group	noncontagious patient

The Ultimate Book of Phonics Word Lists for Grades 3–5 © by Laurie J. Cousseau and Rhonda Graff, Scholastic Inc.

non- Sentences

Believe it or not, some ice cream is nonfat.	We ran nonstop to the finish line.
She was a nonbeliever until she listened to his podcast.	We purchased nontoxic glue for the class art projects.
Molly became a nonfiction writer and journalist.	The nonprofit organization supports many charitable causes.
I'm a nonmember, but I would like to join the club.	The nonresident received a tour of the apartment complex last weekend.
You are speaking absolute nonsense right now, but it is all in good fun.	After flooding, the soccer fields were nonexistent.

dis-: not

The prefix dis- is of Latin origin and means "not." It can also indicate "opposite of," as in like versus dislike. It is an easy prefix to introduce early because it is decodable as a closed syllable.

dis- Words

disable	discomfort	disillusion	displease
disadvantage	disconnect	dislike	dispose
disagree	discontinue	dislocate	dispute
disallow	discord	dislodge	disqualify
disappear	discount	disloyal	disregard
disappoint	discourage	dismantle	disrepair
disapprove	discover	dismiss	disrupt
disarming	discredit	dismount	dissolve
disarray	discuss	disobey	distort
disbelief	disembark	disorderly	distract
discard	disgrace	disown	distrust
disclose	dishearten	dispel	disturb
discolor	dishonest	displace	disuse

dis- Phrases

fell into disrepair	disable the alarm	discolored the shirt
disturbed her brother	completely dishonest	disallow the entry
large disadvantage	sudden disconnect	disobeyed orders
discount store	discontinued item	disagree with her
discuss loudly	dislocated shoulder	extreme dislike
disappearing daylight	dismantled the cabin	disregard for leadership
will discover the truth	disappointed in the results	dispose of the waste

dis- Sentences

Hannah dislikes studying late into the evening.	Can you dispose of the wrappers into the trash can?
My favorite store is having a discount sale this weekend.	Their discussion was too loud, so the teacher asked them to whisper.
Please disregard my message because I was able to solve the problem.	I was disappointed to learn he dropped out of the competition.
Sheila dislocated her shoulder during soccer practice.	Why do my socks always disappear in the laundry?
They discontinued my favorite ice cream flavor.	The loud discussion in the hallway disturbed our class.

mis-: wrong

The prefix mis- is of Latin origin and means "wrong," as in misinterpret. It is an easy prefix to introduce early because it is decodable as a closed syllable.

mis- Words

misaddress	misarrange	misconnect	misdiagnose
misadjust	misbehave	miscopy	misfeed
misadventure	miscalculate	miscue	misfire
misaim	misconception	misdeal	misfit
misalign	misconduct	misdeed	misfortune

The Ultimate Book of Phonics Word Lists for Grades 3–5 © by Laurie J. Cousseau and Rhonda Graff, Scholastic Inc.

mis- Words cont.			
misgiving	mislocate	mispronounce	misstep
misguided	mismanage	misquote	mistake
mishap	mismatch	misread	mistreat
misinterpret	misname	misshapen	mistrial
misjudge	misplace	misspeak	mistrust
mislabel	misplay	misspell	misunderstand
mislead	misprint	misspent	misuse

mis- Phrases

misjudged the distance	misspell words	misbehaving kittens
misinterpret notes	honest mistake	misaligned stones
mismanaged staff	miscopy homework	popular misconception
a mishap while hiking	misquoted statement	misguided decision
mismatched socks	misplayed chess move	misshapen clay pitcher
miscalculated the addition problem	misunderstand the question	misprint in the newspaper

mis- Sentences

Did you miscopy the directions?	My last name is easy to mispronounce.
I might misspell that word because it is so difficult.	Sometimes puppies misbehave to get attention.
Maddy misinterpreted the clues and never found the hidden treasure.	It's a common misconception that bats are blind.
The judge determined a mistrial in the case of the missing jewels.	Rachel misadjusted one of the knobs on the machine, resulting in misalignment.
Lindsey made a spelling mistake on her history exam.	The mishap in the swamp resulted in muddy knees and wet sneakers.
There were many mismatched socks in the basket.	The misshapen clay pot cracked in the hot kiln.
We were unable to finish the trail in one day because of our misguided plans.	The misaligned stones made it difficult to follow the path.

e- / ex-: out or away from

The prefixes e- and ex- are of Latin origin and mean "out." Examples of words incorporating these prefixes are erase and exclude. These prefixes are decodable as an open (e-) or closed (ex-) syllable. The e- can also be pronounced with a schwa, as in erupt.

e-, ex- Words

e-			
eclipse	elapse	eloquent	erect
edict	elate	emerge	erode
edit	elect	emergency	erupt
egregious	elicit	emigrate	evacuate
egress	eliminate	emotion	evade
eject	elite	enormous	evaluate
elaborate	elongate	erase	event

ex-			
exact	exclude	exist	explain
exaggerate	excrete	exit	explore
examination	excuse	exotic	export
example	execute	expanse	expose
excavate	exempt	expect	express
exceed	exercise	expel	extend
excel	exert	expense	exterior
excellent	exhale	experience	exterminate
except	exhausted	experiment	extinct
exchange	exhibit	expert	extra
excite	exile	expire	extreme

e-, ex- Phrases

eject button	president-elect	elaborate plan
elongated shadow	elated scream of joy	erected camping tent
elapsed time	exaggerated drawing	excavated site

e-, ex- Phrases cont.		
art exhibit	exit doorway	conducted a science experiment
finished final exam	daily exercise	exterminated the insects
express concern	excelled at dance	exposed dinosaur bones

e-, ex- Sentences

Who do you think they will elect for class president?	The elaborate plan took months of discussion to finalize.
I can't contain my excitement over the wonderful news.	The story was exaggerated with many unbelievable details.
An excellent chess player studies the game carefully.	Jane came up with an excuse to not participate in gym class.
The science exhibit opens at the museum on Friday night.	The construction crews began to excavate the property yesterday.
I was working on an experiment when the bell rang for lunch.	The exercises in ballet class have elongated my legs.

sub-: below; under

The prefix sub- is of Latin origin and means "below" or "under," as in submarine. It is an easy prefix to introduce early because it is decodable as a closed syllable.

sub- Words

subarctic	sublet	subscribe	subterranean
subconscious	subliminal	subscript	subtext
subculture	submarine	subservient	subtract
subdivision	submerge	subset	subtropics
subdue	submersible	subside	suburban
subfloor	submit	subsidy	suburbs
subgroup	subordinate	substance	subvert
subject	subpar	substandard	subway
subjugate	subplot	substitute	subzero

sub- Phrases

a strong subplot	subtract from the total	submitted his application
main subject	substitute teacher	yellow submarine
subliminal messages	subscribe to a magazine	substandard expectations
subfloor of the building	subarctic temperatures	loud underground subway
will submit my vote	submerged diver	quiet suburbs away from town
subzero temperatures	underwater submersible	subscript notation
glittery substance	suburban location	sublet the apartment
subconscious thoughts	subterranean river	subordinating conjunction

sub- Sentences

He received the message at a subliminal level.	Have you submitted your application yet?
I don't know what subject I will be taking during the first period.	Please subdue the crazy chicken who is squawking wildly.
The frogs are submerged in the pond in the early evening.	In first grade, my teacher taught me how to add and subtract large numbers.
I'm excited to visit New York and ride the subway.	The engineers wanted to build a submarine to learn about the sea floor.
Have you always wanted to live in the suburbs?	I want to subscribe to receive a monthly magazine.
The explorers wore many layers to protect themselves in subzero temperatures.	The valentine was covered with a glittery substance.
A submersible is a smaller underwater vessel than a submarine.	My facial expression sometimes gives away my subconscious thoughts.
The subplot of the movie took place in a yellow submarine.	We explored the subterranean river, which flows beneath the ground.

The Ultimate Book of Phonics Word Lists for Grades 3–5 © by Laurie J. Cousseau and Rhonda Graff. Scholastic Inc.

re-: back; again

The prefix *re-* is of Latin origin and means "back" or "again," as in *return*. It is an easy prefix to introduce early because it is decodable as an open syllable.

re- Words

react	refill	remit	reset
readjust	refinish	remix	respond
reappear	refit	remove	restack
reapply	reflect	rename	restart
reattach	refocus	renew	restate
rebuild	refold	reopen	retell
recall	reform	repack	rethink
recap	refreeze	repaint	retie
recede	refund	repave	retire
receive	refuse	repay	retort
recheck	regain	repel	retrace
recite	regenerate	replace	retract
reconstruct	regroup	replant	retry
recount	rehearse	replay	return
recover	reheat	report	reuse
recur	rejoin	reprint	reveal
recut	relate	reproduce	reverse
recycle	relearn	request	review
redo	release	reread	revise
redraw	reload	rerun	rewind
reduction	relocate	reseal	rewrap
referral	remind	resell	rewrite

re- Phrases

refold laundry	reversible raincoat	reheat dinner
refinish the floors	news reporter	structure rebuild
reprint paperwork	refill vitamins	retract sentence
repaved driveway	football receiver	recited the poem
readjusted rear car mirror	can replant the roses	reminder to be on time
will return the books	rewrite the manuscript	will recycle the cans
will rename the character	repainted the building	renewed our subscription
should retie the knot	had to restart the engine	rejoined the group
receding tide	revised the paragraph	reopened the case

re- Sentences

The red and yellow raincoat was reversible.	I want to rejoin the soccer team this year.
How do you think she will react to winning the contest?	Can we rebuild the barn structure in the back of the property?
We must reprint this stack of pages because there was a spelling mistake.	The poet recited her beautiful poem to celebrate our journey.
When can you rehearse for your role in the school play?	The reporter asked many questions about the new community center.
I refolded the clothes after the laundry basket tipped over.	We had to repave our driveway after the rainstorm destroyed the surface.
The author decided to rename the main character.	They repainted the building because it had faded in the sun.
You should retie the knot, or it will loosen again.	The driver had to restart the engine after the car stalled.
The receding tide will leave seaweed on the shoreline.	The police reopened the case after finding new evidence.

The Ultimate Book of Phonics Word Lists for Grades 3–5 © by Laurie J. Cousseau and Rhonda Graff, Scholastic Inc.

de-: down; away from

The prefix *de-* is of Latin origin and means "down" or "away from," as in *descend*. It is an easy prefix to introduce early because it is decodable as an open syllable.

de- Words

debate	defeat	delight	derange
debug	defense	deliver	descend
decamp	define	demand	describe
decay	deflate	demerit	description
declare	deform	demolish	design
decline	defrost	demonstrate	desire
decode	degrade	denominator	despite
decompose	dehumidify	depart	detach
decrease	dehydrate	depend	determine
decrepit	deject	deplane	dethrone
deduce	delay	deplete	detract
deface	delicious	derail	devour

de- Phrases

depending on the weather	determine the winner	can deflate the tires
debate team	devour breakfast	demand answers
declined appointment	clear description	deliver packages
dehydrated athlete	delicious apples	demonstrate kindness
decreasing numbers	decoded secret code	descending staircase
denominator in a fraction	demolish the old building	delayed the event
decrepit building	defrosted the windows	has a strong defense
despite the obstacles	will depart at noon	was delighted to see her

de- Sentences

Can you define your design ideas for this upcoming project?	The team was defeated in the playoffs, but they were proud of their season.
The dehydrated athletes stopped to drink water and have fruit.	Katie made the most delicious cupcakes last weekend.
Can you describe the cotton sweatshirt you found?	How do I determine who has the right answer?
I will deliver several meals to your house later this evening.	Can you decode the hidden message in the bottle?
I depend upon my dog to cuddle with me every night.	I want to devour my birthday cake, but that is not polite.

pre-: before

The suffixes *pre-* and *per-* (page 81) have similar-sounding pronunciations, so students often get them confused. They are both of Latin origin. The prefix *pre-* means "before," as in *predict*. *Pre-* is an easy prefix to introduce early because it is decodable as an open syllable.

pre- Words

preamble	pregame	prepay	preside
prearrange	preheat	preplan	presume
precaution	prejudge	preproduction	preteen
precede	prelaunch	prequalify	pretend
precept	preliminary	prerinse	pretest
precook	preload	presale	pretext
precut	prelude	preschool	pretreat
predate	premier	prescribe	pretrial
predict	premix	prescription	prevent
preface	preoccupy	presell	preview
prefix	preorder	preserve	previous
preform	preowned	preset	prewash

The Ultimate Book of Phonics Word Lists for Grades 3–5 © by Laurie J. Cousseau and Rhonda Graff, Scholastic Inc.

pre- Phrases

precooked food	preliminary decision	preceding events
prescribe sunshine	preheated dinner	prepay for the meal
preoccupied mind	doctor's prescription	prevent damages
predated application	preamble to the novel	take careful precautions
pretending to be on an adventure	predict the future	prefix at the beginning of the word

pre- Sentences

The preheated dinner did not taste fresh.	Can I prepay for the rented kayaks?
I predicted the end of the film based upon the foreshadowing of events.	The preamble to the novel provided clues about the ending.
We stopped at the pharmacy to pick up the doctor's prescription.	The prediction for the future held promise for peace.
We took careful precautions packing for our long rafting adventure.	We pretended to be balloonists traveling around the world in 80 days.
I would prescribe a nice dose of sunshine after long winter days.	"I presume that you are right," Watson said to the detective.

per-: through

Since the suffixes per- and pre- (page 80) have similar-sound pronunciations, students often confuse them. They are both of Latin origin. The prefix per- means "through," as in perforate. Per- is an easy prefix to introduce early because it is decodable as an r-controlled syllable.

per- Words

perceive	perforce	permanent	personal
percent	perform	permeate	perspire
perceptive	perfume	permit	persuade
perchance	perfunctory	perpendicular	persuasion
percussion	perimeter	perpetual	pertain
perennial	perhaps	perplex	perturb
perfect	perish	persevere	pervade
perforate	perjury	persist	pervert

The Ultimate Book of Phonics Word Lists for Grades 3–5 © by Laurie J. Cousseau and Rhonda Graff, Scholastic Inc.

per- Phrases

perpendicular lines	small percent	personal decision
perplexing problem	perfect house	permanent home
percussion instruments	sweet perfume	persevering spirit
perennial gardens	perfunctory response	pervading atmosphere
outside perimeter of the yard	perspired during exercise	amazing circus performance

per- Sentences

My favorite perfume has a floral scent.	He used a can opener to perforate the lid.
The perennial gardens bloom every year in the late spring.	The pervading atmosphere is one of doom and gloom.
The wedding near the coast was absolutely perfect.	We walked around the perimeter of the house to check the foundation.
They donated 25 percent of the proceeds of the lemonade stand.	The vertical line was perpendicular to the horizontal line.
The hikers perspired in the direct sunlight with no shade.	She demonstrated a persevering spirit when climbing Mount Everest.
The unsolved case of the missing brownies was perplexing.	Percy's performance with percussion instruments was inspiring.

pro-: forward

The prefix *pro-* is of Latin origin and means "forward," as in *proceed*. It is an easy prefix to introduce early because it is decodable as an open syllable. *Pro-* can have a long or short sound in the word, depending on whether it is a verb or a noun, as in *project/project* or *progress/progress*.

pro- Words

proactive	proclaim	professional	profuse
procedure	procrastinate	professor	program
proceed	procure	profile	progress
process	produce	profit	prohibit
procession	profess	profound	project

The Ultimate Book of Phonics Word Lists for Grades 3–5 © by Laurie J. Cousseau and Rhonda Graff, Scholastic Inc.

pro- Words cont.			
prolific	propel	proscribe	protract
prologue	prophecy	prosecute	protrude
prolong	prophet	prospect	proverb
prominent	proportion	protect	provide
pronoun	propose	protegee	provision
pronounce	propulsion	proton	provoke

pro- Phrases

biology professor	provided an excuse	prolonged vacation
project on the screen	security protection	easy procedure
hired professional musicians	local produce	proceed forward
procrastinated for weeks	balanced proportions	ample provisions
expressed profuse apologies	huge progress	profile of the artist

pro- Sentences

The class project was finally complete.	Eat your meals in balanced proportions.
We get fresh produce at the local farmer's market.	The vast proportion of the work is complete.
We packed ample provisions for the car ride.	I procured two bottles of water for the hike.
She charted the progress of her experiment on a graph.	There were profuse apologies for the late delivery.
The science professor gave an interesting talk about endangered animals.	The prologue was an introduction to the events of the novel.
Since we haven't seen our relatives in a long time, we prolonged our visit.	I wear kneepads to protect my knees when I go roller-skating.
The professional basketball player was recruited for a new league.	He stayed calm and didn't want to provoke the bear.
Paula procrastinated for weeks but completed her project in a single day!	Let's prolong our vacation on this gorgeous island.

uni-: one / *bi-:* two / *tri-:* three

You can teach this set of prefixes together as they relate to numbers. *Uni-* means "one," as in *unicycle. Bi-* means "two," as in *bicycle. Tri-* means "three," as in *tricycle.*

uni-, bi-, tri- Words

uni-			
unicellular	unify	unisex	univalve
unicorn	unilateral	unison	universal
unicycle	union	unit	universe
uniform	unique	unite	university

bi-			
biannual	bicuspid	billion	biplane
biathlon	bicycle	bimonthly	bipolar
bicentennial	biennial	binary	biracial
biceps	bifocals	binoculars	bisect
bicoastal	bilateral	bipartisan	bivalve
bicolor	bilingual	biped	biweekly

tri-			
triad	triceps	trident	trio
triangle	tricolor	triennial	triple
triathlon	tricorn	trillion	triplet
trice	tricycle	trilogy	tripod

uni-, bi-, tri- Phrases

united in their decision	universal studios	rainbow unicorn
expanding universe	band uniform	unified front
new birding binoculars	pink bicycle	flexed biceps
bilingual speaker	bivalve organism	bimonthly meeting
Neptune's trident	tricolor painting	movie trilogy
camera tripod	triangular shape	tricycle with a basket

The Ultimate Book of Phonics Word Lists for Grades 3–5 © by Laurie J. Cousseau and Rhonda Graff, Scholastic Inc.

uni-, bi-, tri- Sentences

The colors of your uniform are colorful and bright.	Would it be fun to learn how to ride a unicycle?
My little sister sleeps with her rainbow unicorn every night.	Sometimes I look up at the night sky and wonder how big the universe is.
I love to go bird-watching with my new binoculars.	Uncle Ben needs bifocals to read the small print.
I have been going to the gym weekly to strengthen my biceps.	Bella's bicycle with the tricolor basket is quite fabulous!
Travis likes riding his tricycle on the boardwalk.	The house in the mountains is shaped like a triangle.
The movie trilogy features Neptune and his famous trident.	Phil left his phone on the tripod to film the band.

ante-: before / anti-: against

The prefixes ante- and anti- are of Latin origin. Both are pronounced /antə/ but have different meanings. The prefix ante- means "before," as in the word antecedent. The prefix anti- means "against," as in the word antidote. Since they are pronounced the same, students often confuse them. Learning the meaning of each prefix will help students choose the correct spelling.

ante-, anti- Words

ante-			
antebellum	antechamber	antediluvian	anteroom
antecedent	antedate	anterior	
anti-			
antibacterial	antifreeze	antioxidant	antithesis
antibiotic	antigravity	antiracism	antitoxin
antibody	antihero	antiseptic	antitrust
anticlimactic	antihistamine	antisocial	antivenom
antidote	antinausea	antiterrorism	antivirus

ante-, anti- Phrases

anteroom of the hotel	anterior door	the antechamber of the castle
previous antecedent	villainous antihero	disease-fighting antibodies
unfriendly and antisocial	antihistamine for allergies	blue antifreeze
antibiotic medicine	anticlimactic movie	antigravity machine
applied antiseptic to the scrape	antibacterial cream for germs	precious antidote for the poison

ante-, anti- Sentences

The antecedent in the sentence for Beth is the pronoun *her*.	The right ventricle is the anterior part of the heart.
She injured the anterior part of her shoulder.	The hatch opened into a small antechamber that led into the main hall.
Wash your hands with antibacterial soap.	It was an anticlimactic finish to the match.
Laughter is a perfect antidote for stress.	The antithesis to anger is acceptance.
The nurse treated the patient's allergies with antihistamine.	Do you have enough antifreeze in the engine?
In the movie, the precious antidote for the poison was found just in time.	The astronauts entered the antigravity chamber.
The villainous antihero was a foil for the protagonist in the epic tale.	The doctor gave him an antivenom injection for the snake bite.
The nurse used antiseptic on her scraped knee.	We floated and danced in the air in the antigravity machine.

The Ultimate Book of Phonics Word Lists for Grades 3–5 © by Laurie J. Cousseau and Rhonda Graff, Scholastic Inc.

Roots

Roots carry the most meaning in a word. They are primarily of Latin origin. In addition, the root often carries the accent or stress when we pronounce a word. It can have a short-vowel sound, as in *rupt*, *dict*, and *ject*. It can also have a long-vowel sound, as in *duce*, *vide*, and *vise*.

Roots are often "bound" morphemes, which means they do not make a word unless they are combined with an affix (prefix or suffix). For example, *spect* ("to look") is not a word on its own unless it is combined with a prefix, such as *in-* to make the word *inspect*. It can also be joined with a suffix, such as *-ate*, to make the word *spectate*. Many words can be formed by adding prefixes and suffixes to bound roots. Word-building activities enhance vocabulary development and help students improve their spelling.

There are more than a hundred commonly used roots in the English language, but we focused on a few high-utility roots. You can teach roots as an associative group organized around meaning. For example, students will see the value of learning roots associated with parts of the body, such as *dict* ("to speak") and *aud* ("to hear"). Another group of roots relate to motion (see pages 96–103), such as *rupt* ("to break") and *ject* ("to throw").

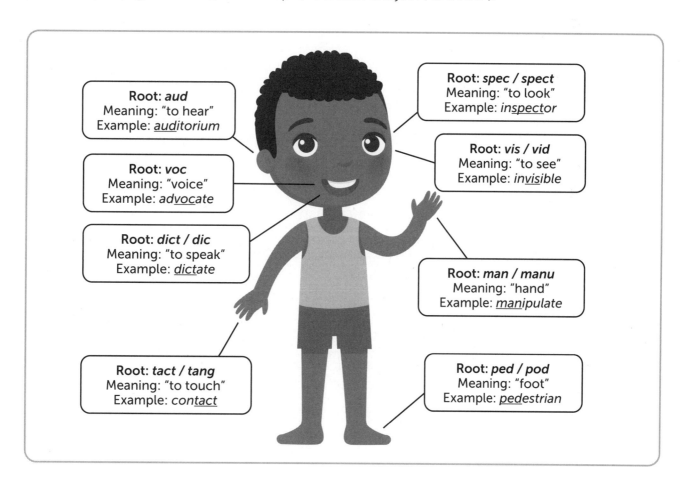

Root: *aud*
Meaning: "to hear"
Example: <u>aud</u>itorium

Root: *voc*
Meaning: "voice"
Example: ad<u>voc</u>ate

Root: *dict / dic*
Meaning: "to speak"
Example: <u>dict</u>ate

Root: *tact / tang*
Meaning: "to touch"
Example: con<u>tact</u>

Root: *spec / spect*
Meaning: "to look"
Example: in<u>spect</u>or

Root: *vis / vid*
Meaning: "to see"
Example: in<u>vis</u>ible

Root: *man / manu*
Meaning: "hand"
Example: <u>man</u>ipulate

Root: *ped / pod*
Meaning: "foot"
Example: <u>ped</u>estrian

spect / spec: to look

Spect and spec are two forms of the same root, which means "to look," as in inspect and special. Both roots are of Latin origin. A few words contain spic, which is a less-common variation, as in conspicuous.

spect, spec Words

spect		
aspect	perspective	spectacle
circumspect	prospect	spectacular
disrespectful	prospector	spectator
inspect	respect	specter
inspection	respectful	spectrum
inspector	retrospect	suspect
introspection	retrospective	unsuspecting
spec, spic		
conspicuous	specialty	specify
especially	species	specimen
inconspicuous	specific	speculate
special	specification	

spect, spec Phrases

inspect the box	spectrum of color	in retrospect, he thought
disrespectful comment	unsuspecting friend	respectful silence
careful inspection	spectacular show	speculate carefully
special clothing	very specific details	inspected the basement
narrow perspective	loyal spectators at the game	rounded up the suspects
artist's retrospective	wore round spectacles	inconspicuous clothes

spect, spec Sentences

We reviewed every aspect of the plan.	I suspect the missing desserts have been eaten.

The Ultimate Book of Phonics Word Lists for Grades 3–5 © by Laurie J. Cousseau and Rhonda Graff, Scholastic Inc.

spect, spec Sentences cont.	
The directors were very circumspect in their statements.	Ellis experienced a whole spectrum of emotions during the inspection.
The teacher gave specific directions for the homework assignment.	After the flood, the inspector checked everything over carefully.
The inconspicuous inspector wore round spectacles.	We speculated about the motive behind missing desserts.
Being respectful is an important character trait.	The view from the top of the mountain is spectacular.
Larry did not specify a reason for leaving the lecture.	A disrespectful tone and comment can hurt someone's feelings.

vis / vid: to see

Vis and vid are two forms of the same root, which means "to see," as in vision or evidence. Both roots are of Latin origin.

vis, vid Words

vis			
advise	provision	visage	visit
advisor	revise	viscosity	visitor
devise	revision	visibility	visor
envision	supervise	visible	vista
improvise	supervisor	vision	visual
invisible	television	visionary	visualize
vid			
evidence	provide	video	videotape
evident	provident	videocam	vivid

vis, vid Phrases

college advisor	television show	provide healthy snacks
invisible in a crowd	yearly visitors	annual doctor's visit
visualize winning	solid evidence	evident facts

vis, vid Phrases cont.		
packed camping provisions	a visionary outlook	envision a bright future
vistas of snow-covered mountains	completed revisions on the essay	providential good fortune

vis, vid Sentences

Do we have a visual of the astronauts?	The solid evidence will prove their theory.
You have a surprise visitor at the front door.	How visible is the scar on my knee?
The character's special powers made him invisible.	Let me provide you with water before you walk home.
How long has that television series been streaming?	Visualize winning the event, and it will happen!
I envision us working together again on numerous projects.	She wore a visor to protect her eyes from the harsh sunlight.
The visionary leader used evidence to visualize a promising future.	Viola revised her essay and included evidence to support her claim.
Last weekend, we had a wonderful visit at Grandma's house.	We took a video of our new puppy playing in the snow.
A wind advisory prevented us from going on a hike.	Viscosity is a measure of how liquid flows at certain temperatures.

aud: to hear

The root aud is of Latin origin and means "to hear," as in audible.

aud Words

audible	audiobook	audit	auditorium
audience	audiology	audition	auditory
audio	audiovisual	auditor	inaudible

aud Phrases

engaging audience	louder audio	inaudible whisper
tax audit	bank auditor	audiovisual class

The Ultimate Book of Phonics Word Lists for Grades 3–5 © by Laurie J. Cousseau and Rhonda Graff, Scholastic Inc.

aud Phrases cont.		
perfect audition	packed auditorium	audiology services
prefers audiobooks	audible static and noise	auditory interference

aud Sentences

She had a fantastic audition for drama school.	The teacher used an audiobook to share the story.
The auditorium holds more than a thousand people.	She spoke softly in an almost inaudible whisper.
The audience was lively last night in the packed auditorium.	The school will buy new audiovisual equipment.
The audio of the audition was very crackly and hard to hear.	The teacher turned up the audio on the computer so that we could hear.
The company had an unexpected audit.	Audiology services helped determine the patient's hearing.

dict / dic: to speak

Dict and *dic* are two forms of the same root, which means "to speak," as in *dictate* and *dedicate*. Both roots are of Latin origin.

dict, dic Words

dict			
addictive	dictation	edict	prediction
contradict	dictator	malediction	unpredictable
contradiction	diction	predict	valedictorian
dictate	dictionary	predictable	verdict
dic			
dedicate	indicate	predicament	vindicate

dict, dic Phrases

clear contradiction	English dictionary	false prediction
dictated conversation	predicting the future	indicate the location
clear diction	predictable outcome	unpredictable weather

dict, dic Sentences

Clear diction is vital for a public speaker.	Dark skies indicated an upcoming storm.
After reading the first chapter, we were asked to make a prediction.	Is it too early to predict a result in the election?
The angry boy contradicted what his brother said.	In March, the weather is much less predictable.
The teacher dictated sentences for students to write in their notebooks.	A snowy summer day is a contradiction in terms.
Sometimes I look up words in the dictionary to clarify their definition.	The fairy tale began with a malediction, but the heroine reversed the curse.

voc / vok: voice

Voc and *vok* are two forms of the same root, which means "voice," as in *vocal* and *evoke*. Both roots are of Latin origin.

voc, vok Words

voc			
advocacy	invocate	provocative	vocalist
advocate	invocation	unequivocal	vocalize
equivocal	irrevocable	vocabulary	vocation
evocative	provocation	vocal	vociferous

vok			
evoke	invoke	provoke	revoke

voc, vok Phrases

evoke emotions	provoke change for good	irrevocable turn of events
advocate for justice	vocal artist	advocacy group
solo vocalist	vocalize opinions	equivocal mood
invoke a feeling of cooperation	invocation at the ceremony	vocabulary word of the day

The Ultimate Book of Phonics Word Lists for Grades 3–5 © by Laurie J. Cousseau and Rhonda Graff, Scholastic Inc.

voc, vok Sentences

Fresh, juicy peaches evoke memories of summer.	Vocalize your opinions now, or we will move on to the next subject.
The parents and students advocated for a new playground.	Theo wanted to see if he could provoke a strong reaction from me.
The community invoked the mayor's help to improve the local park.	The advocacy group helped us reach our goals.
This may be an irrevocable step in the wrong direction.	The results of the investigation were equivocal and uncertain.
After getting a part in the school play, I decided to take some vocal lessons.	The lead vocalist sang four songs during the performance.

tact / tang: to touch

Tact and *tang* are two forms of the same root, which means "to touch," as in *contact* and *tangible*. Both roots are of Latin origin.

tact, tang Words

tact			
contact	tact	tactic	tactile
intact	tactful	tactician	tactless
tang			
disentangle	tangent	tangible	tangram
entangle	tangential	tangle	untangle
intangible			

tact, tang Phrases

contact lens	intangible results	tactless comments
tangential thought	persuasive tactics	untangled the knots
intact concept	skilled tactician	entangled in the yarn
tactful friend	contacted by mail	a tactile memory
tangled and twisted string	tactile sticky surface	off on a tangent

The Ultimate Book of Phonics Word Lists for Grades 3–5 © by Laurie J. Cousseau and Rhonda Graff, Scholastic Inc.

tact, tang Sentences

The school will contact our families about the upcoming trip.	Max is a master tactician at the game of chess.
The old house had an intangible feeling of warmth and coziness.	Tony made a tactless remark, which he later regretted.
Sara lost a contact lens, so she had to wear her eyeglasses.	Our fishing lines became tangled up in the water.
I dropped my phone, but luckily it stayed intact and did not shatter.	When the young child was telling her story, she kept going off on tangents.
The spy used secret tactics to locate the suspect.	The hands-on science museum offered many wonderful tactile experiences.

man / manu: hand

Man and *manu* are two forms of the same root, which means "hand," as in *manicure* and *manual*. Both roots are of Latin origin.

man, manu Words

man			
emancipate	manager	manicure	manipulate
manage	mandate	manifest	manipulation
manageable	mandatory	manifestation	manner
management	maneuver	manifesto	

manu			
manual	manufacture	manufacturing	manuscript

man, manu Phrases

handwritten manuscript	manual labor	manufacturing plant
managed the students	manager in training	nail manicure
maneuvered the sailboat	manufacture bicycle parts	manifested positive results
mandatory attendance	very polite manners	upper-level management
followed a stern mandate	manipulation of the evidence	manifesto of requests

The Ultimate Book of Phonics Word Lists for Grades 3–5 © by Laurie J. Cousseau and Rhonda Graff, Scholastic Inc.

man, manu Sentences

Manual labor can be very rewarding.	The factory manufactured automobile parts.
The toddler manipulated the blocks to build a tower.	Meg enjoyed a manicure and having her nails painted a bright color.
At basketball practice, the coach taught us new maneuvers.	Her words and actions manifested positive results.
Manuel typed the handwritten manuscript and then edited it.	The amount of work required is very manageable.

ped / pod: foot

Ped and *pod* are two forms of the same root, which means "foot," as in *centipede* and *tripod*. Both roots are of Latin origin.

ped, pod Words

ped			
backpedal	expedition	pedal	pedicab
biped	impede	peddle	pedicure
centipede	impediment	peddler	pedigree
expedient	millipede	pedestal	pedometer
expedite	moped	pedestrian	quadruped

pod			
gastropod	octopod	podiatry	tripod
monopod	podiatrist	podium	unipod

ped, pod Phrases

crawling centipede	wooden pedestal	science expedition
walked with a pedometer	camera tripod	impediment to progress
pedicure appointment	podiatrist's office	silver, sporty moped
rode on a pedicab	spinning pedals	pedestrian crossing
eight-legged octopod	podium for the lecture	squirming millipede with many legs

ped, pod Sentences

Elephants and horses are quadrupeds, which means they have four legs.	Simon set off on a scientific expedition to study centipedes.
Penny made an appointment with the podiatrist because her feet hurt.	Don't let a small argument impede our progress.
The championship soccer team placed their trophy on the pedestal.	Sage hopped on her silver moped and raced to the festival.
She pressed her foot on the gas pedal, and the car accelerated.	The pedestrians crossed the street when the flashing light turned green.
Piper has a pedicure appointment once a month.	Parker needed to use a step ladder to see over the podium.

ject: to throw

The root *ject* is of Latin origin and means "to throw," as in *eject*.

ject Words

adjective	inject	objection	reject
conjecture	injection	objective	rejection
dejected	interject	project	subject
dejection	interjection	projection	subjective
eject	object	projector	trajectory

ject Phrases

small object	history project	rejected opinion
sharp interjection	her favorite subject	ejected from the game
feeling of dejection	old film projector	painful injection
raised an objection	followed the trajectory	clearly stated objectives
conjecture and guess	descriptive adjectives	dejected expression
objected to the statement	projected the image	subjective conclusion

The Ultimate Book of Phonics Word Lists for Grades 3–5 © by Laurie J. Cousseau and Rhonda Graff, Scholastic Inc.

jectSentences

Rejection can lead to new beginnings.	The light projected dancing shadows on the wall.
The sad boy looked dejected, but his friends cheered him up.	His objective was not to win the soccer tournament, but to enjoy the game.
They ejected themselves from the plane while skydiving.	My mom did not object to my request for a sleepover.
Please do not interject when others are speaking.	Whether there is a sea monster is open to conjecture.
There are many adjectives to describe the object you are holding.	Choose an interesting subject for the upcoming history project.

mot / mov: to move

Mot and mov are two forms of the same root, which means "to move," as in motor and move. Both roots are of Latin origin.

mot, mov Words

mot			
automotive	emotion	motion	motorboat
commotion	locomotive	motivate	promote
demote	locomotion	motive	promotion
demotion	motel	motocross	remote
emote	motif	motor	
mov			
immovable	move	movie	remove
movable	movement	removal	unmoved

mot, mov Phrases

strong emotions	forward motion	promotes positivity
loud commotion	motivate change	remote for the TV
historic motel	motocross champion	automotive repair
emote a sense of calm	noisy locomotive engine	motorboat race
central motif of the movie	immovable machine parts	movable puzzle pieces
unmoved from the spot	demoted from his position	questionable motives

mot, mov Sentences

The central motif in the movie is finding joy.	Her kind facial expression emotes a sense of calm.
We saw many unique cars at the automotive show.	Morgan made a motion for me to move away from the doorway.
The speaker's voice was low and shaky with emotion.	The historic motel had a vacancy for the next few nights.
The train was pulled by an electric locomotive.	Lorna is motivated to promote her new book remotely.
Megan moved to a small remote town next to a motel.	The athletes were motivated to win after a successful practice.
I heard a loud commotion in the street during the motocross championship.	My family will be moving to a new home at the end of the school year.
The donkey remained unmoved from the edge of the field.	The motion sensor detected an animal next to the house.
The volunteer for that position has questionable motives.	The actor showed strong emotions during the final scene.
The speedy motorboat zipped across the lake, creating a wave.	Promoting positivity creates a climate of optimism.

pend: to hang

The root *pend* is of Latin origin and means "to hang," as in *suspend*.

pend Words

append	dependent	independence	pendulum
appendage	depending	independent	perpendicular
appendix	expend	interdependent	stupendous
compendium	expenditure	pendant	suspend
depend	impending	pending	suspenders

pend Phrases

pending decision	impending storm	a compendium of stories
silver pendant	suspend your disbelief	perpendicular lines
independent student	red suspenders	depended on her friends
swinging pendulum	broken appendage	interdependent ideas
appendix of the book	expend a lot of energy	dependent child
stupendous performance	depending on the results	fight for independence

pend Sentences

I am dependent upon my best friends for support.	The red suspenders helped hold up her canvas pants.
Ivy feels independent when she goes to the market by herself.	Draw a line perpendicular to the base of the form.
Prices vary for produce depending upon the time of year.	Everyone was in awe of her stupendous performance.
Pet owners and their pets have an interdependent relationship.	The appendix is found at the back of the book.
The referee suspended the game due to a pending storm.	The pendulum of the large clock swung back and forth.
We waited in suspense for the impending decision.	Sophie adored the silver pendant she received for her birthday.

The Ultimate Book of Phonics Word Lists for Grades 3–5 © by Laurie J. Cousseau and Rhonda Graff, Scholastic Inc.

port: to carry

The root *port* is of Latin origin and means "to carry," as in *transport*.

port Words

airport	import	passport	report
comport	important	portable	seaport
comportment	imported	portage	support
deport	importune	portal	teleport
deportation	inopportune	porter	transport
export	opportune	portfolio	transportation
heliport	opportunity	portico	transporter

port Phrases

stuck at the airport	opportune moments	passenger's passport
import handwoven fabric	perfect opportunity	public transportation
portable stove	exported goods	carried an art portfolio
at the heliport	magical portal	opportunity to succeed
porter at the hotel	finished my report	landed at the seaport
provided extra support	transported cargo by truck	circular portico at the entrance

port Sentences

How do you export contacts onto your new phone?	Oscar couldn't have arrived at a less opportune moment.
Parker needs the opportunity to do more work on his art portfolio.	They are building a heliport on the island to import and export produce.
Write the important information about the quiz in your planners.	The airport was congested during the holiday weekend.
They have a tremendous opportunity to visit the seaport.	The moving truck transported the bulk of our furniture.
We transported our canoe to the landing near the river.	We shared our assignments through the classroom portal.

The Ultimate Book of Phonics Word Lists for Grades 3–5 © by Laurie J. Cousseau and Rhonda Graff, Scholastic Inc.

rupt: to break

The root *rupt* is of Latin origin and means "to break," as in *rupture.*

rupt Words

abrupt	corrupt	disruption	incorrupt
abruptly	corruptible	disruptive	interrupt
bankrupt	corruption	erupt	interruption
bankruptcy	disrupt	eruption	rupture

rupt Phrases

abrupt stop	about to erupt	interrupted by mistake
abruptly stated	disrupted meeting	ruptured pipes
bankrupt company	volcanic eruption	brief interruption
declared bankruptcy	corrupt files	disruptive noise

rupt Sentences

The loud noise outside disrupted the class.	We interrupt this show to bring you an important news flash.
We abruptly stopped talking when the teacher entered the room.	The game continued after a brief interruption due to rain.
The team worked hard to prevent the company from going bankrupt.	Ruptured pipes caused a sudden noise that disrupted the silence.
The picnic was disrupted by thunderstorms and lightning.	I need a quiet room where I can work without interruption.
Although the volcano has not been active for 25 years, it erupted abruptly.	An abrupt change in plans disrupted our trip.
The disruptive noise made it very hard to sleep without constantly waking up.	The corrupted files damaged my laptop computer.

struct: to build

The root *struct* is of Latin origin and means "to build," as in *construct*.

struct Words

construct	destructive	instructive	reconstruction
construction	indestructible	instructor	substructure
deconstruct	infrastructure	obstruct	structural
destruct	instruct	obstruction	structure
destruction	instruction	reconstruct	unstructured

struct Phrases

instruct the class	instructive lesson	unstructured playtime
destruction from the storm	obstructed the road	instruction manual
a wooden structure	reconstruction plans	destructive winds
active construction zone	trained a new instructor	obstruct the view
obstruction on the hiking path	constructed a bridge out of straws	structural damage after the earthquake

struct Sentences

The entire structure needs to be reconstructed.	Fallen trees obstructed the path to the pond.
The carpenter called in her construction team to get the project started.	The teacher provided clear instructions for our homework assignment.
The avalanche left a trail of destruction and obstructed the road.	There were plans to reconstruct the historic structure in town.
The game came with an instruction manual, but I didn't need it.	The art teacher is instructing the class on different ways to hold a paintbrush.
They plan to construct a community center behind the house.	Lily's favorite instructor provided her a homework pass.

tract: to pull

The root *tract* is of Latin origin and means "to pull," as in *tractor*.

tract Words

abstract	contractor	extract	retractable
attract	contractual	extraction	retraction
attraction	detract	intractable	subtract
attractive	detractor	protracted	subtraction
contract	distract	protractor	traction
contraction	distraction	retract	tractor

tract Phrases

abstract art	distracting noises	printed a retraction
attract positivity	contracted a muscle	large red tractor
attractive artwork	extracted honey	teaches subtraction
intractable position	vanilla extract for baking	building contractor
lost traction on a bike	magnetic attraction	provided a distraction
use a protractor	subtract the numbers	a retractable pen

tract Sentences

The buzzing fly distracted the students.	There will be subtraction problems on the test.
The contract was finally completed.	We extracted fresh honey from the beehive.
Hadley mowed the lawn on the tractor.	He used a retractable pen to write his essay.
The cake recipe calls for vanilla extract.	The attractive puppy has shiny golden fur.
The tractor pull at the fair attracts many visitors.	The abstract art gallery is full of attractive masterpieces.
I tried to distract him from the dangling spiders.	The bicycle tires lost traction on the slippery road.
Think positively and you will attract good things.	The contractor used subtraction to find the correct measurement.
The farmer parked the large red tractor in the barn.	The colorful flowers and clover attract bees who extract nectar and pollen.

Find the Root

Give students practice in identifying roots with this strategic game.

Number of Players: 2

You'll Need: Find the Root game board (page 105) • 2 different-colored pencils

Setting Up the Game

Make a copy of the blank Find the Root game board. Decide on specific roots you want students to target (for example, *tract, pend,* and *ject*). Find the corresponding word lists in the book and choose words for the game. Write one word in each box of the game board. Be sure to include prefixes and suffixes.

Make a copy of the game board for each player. Provide each player with a different-colored pencil to use for the entire game.

Find the Root			
at<u>tract</u>	pendant	distraction	re<u>ject</u>ed
subject	per<u>pend</u>icular	contraction	con<u>tract</u>
dependable	<u>tract</u>or	ob<u>ject</u>ing	impending
e<u>ject</u>ed	suspend	pro<u>ject</u>or	ex<u>tract</u>

How to Play

1. Players take turns choosing a word from the board and underlining its root. After choosing a word, players read the root first in isolation and then the entire word. Then they color in the box with their pencil.

2. The goal of the game is to get four boxes in a row—horizontally, vertically, or diagonally—so players must be strategic in choosing words at each turn.

3. Players continue taking turns choosing words and coloring boxes.

4. The first person to color in four boxes in a row wins. The player must read all the words on the board correctly to win.

Going Further

• Challenge students to define the words based on known prefixes, suffixes, and roots. As a bonus, have players use a word from the game board in a sentence.

• For additional fluency practice, have students take home copies of the game to play with their families. Encourage players to read the columns multiple times.

Find the Root

The Ultimate Book of Phonics Word Lists for Grades 3–5 © by Laurie J. Cousseau and Rhonda Graff, Scholastic Inc.

In the Doghouse

Players race to the doghouse as they combine base words with prefixes or suffixes to form new words.

Number of Players: 2 to 4

You'll Need: Bone Cards (page 107) • In the Doghouse game board (pages 108–109) • blank Base Word Cards (page 110) • scissors • tape • file folder (optional) • game pieces (e.g., buttons, coins) • die

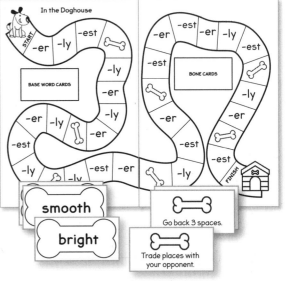

Setting Up the Game

Make a copy of the blank In the Doghouse game board. Decide on specific prefixes/suffixes you want students to target (for example, the suffixes *-er, -est,* and *-ly*). We recommend choosing between two to four prefixes/suffixes to make the game more manageable for students.

In each space on the game board, write one of the target prefixes/suffixes. Make copies of both pages of the game board for each group of players. To assemble the game board, fold or cut along the dotted line (B) and tape (B) to (A) as indicated. (Optional: Tape the game board to the inside of a file folder to make it sturdier.)

Photocopy the Base Word Cards and the Bone Cards onto cardstock. Make as many copies of the blank Base Word Cards as needed. Find the corresponding word lists in the book and choose base words that can be joined with the prefixes/suffixes on the game board. Write the words on the blank Base Word Cards. **Note:** Make sure all the base words work with <u>all</u> the prefixes/suffixes on the board since players will be choosing random cards.

Cut apart all the game cards, including the Bone Cards. Shuffle the Base Word Cards and stack them face down on the game board where indicated. Do the same with the Bone Cards. Provide each player with a game piece and give each group a die.

How to Play

1. Players take turns rolling the die and moving their game piece accordingly.
   - If players land on a prefix/suffix, they pick a card from the Base Word Card pile. Players must join the base word together with the prefix/suffix and read the word aloud. (**Note:** If possible, have an adult present to check players' accuracy in putting together and reading the word.)
   - If players land on a bone, they pick a card from the Bone Card pile and follow the directions.
2. Players continue taking turns until a player reaches the Doghouse.
3. The first player to reach the Doghouse wins the game.

Going Further

For additional practice, make extra copies of the game board for students to take home and play with their families.

The Ultimate Book of Phonics Word Lists for Grades 3–5 © by Laurie J. Cousseau and Rhonda Graff, Scholastic Inc.

Bone Cards

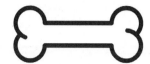

Go back 3 spaces.

Take an extra turn.

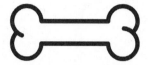

Skip a turn.

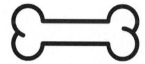

Take an extra turn.

Go back 1 space.

Move ahead
2 spaces.

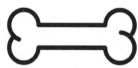

Trade places with
your opponent.

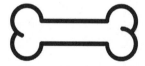

Trade places with
your opponent.

Move ahead
3 spaces.

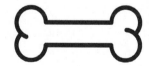

Go back 1 space.

Skip a turn.

Move ahead
2 spaces.

In the Doghouse

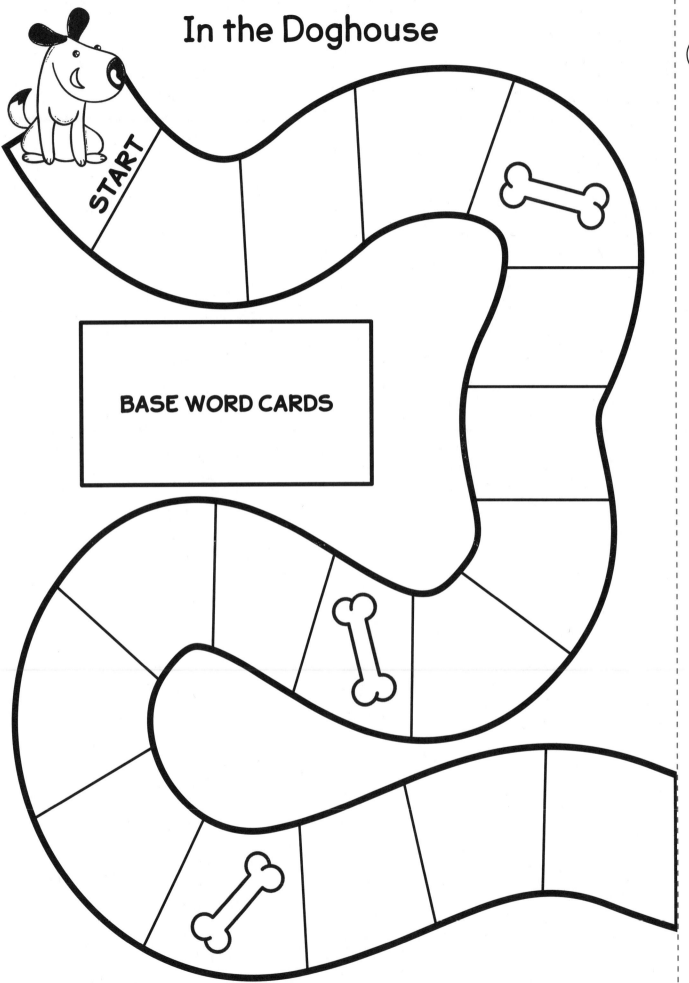

START

BASE WORD CARDS

Attach page Ⓑ here. Line up game board.

B

Fold or cut on dotted line. Attach to page **A**.

BONE CARDS

FINISH

The Ultimate Book of Phonics Word Lists for Grades 3–5 © by Laurie J. Cousseau and Rhonda Graff, Scholastic Inc.

Base Word Cards

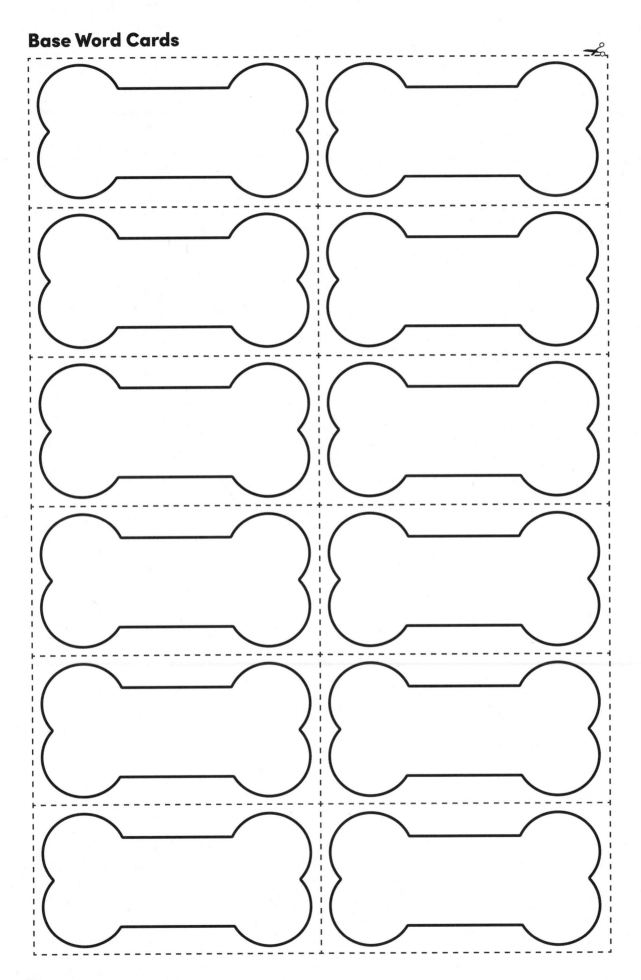

The Ultimate Book of Phonics Word Lists for Grades 3–5 © by Laurie J. Cousseau and Rhonda Graff, Scholastic Inc.

Suffix Flip-Book

Students build vocabulary skills as they fill up their flip-book with words that use target suffixes and determine the words' definitions.

You'll Need: Base Word Cards (page 112) • Suffix Flip-Book (page 113) • Suffix Spinner (page 114) • pencil and paper clip (for the spinner) • scissors • glue • pencils • small paper bag

_____'s Suffix Flip-Book	
graceful	full of grace
hopeless	without hope
power	
care	
cheer	
spot	

Setting Up the Game

Make a copy of the blank Base Word Cards. Decide on specific suffixes you want students to target (for example, *-ful* and *-less*). Choose two suffixes that pair well with each other. Find the corresponding word lists in the book and choose words for the game. On the blank word cards, write base words that work with the chosen suffixes. Make sure all chosen base words work with both suffixes. Cut apart the cards and place them in a small paper bag.

Make a copy of the blank Suffix Flip-Book for each student. Fold the flip-books in half lengthwise. Cut the dotted lines up to the center fold. (Option: You can have students do these steps when they get ready to play.)

Make a copy of the Suffix Spinner and write your chosen suffixes in the four sections; each suffix will have two sections. Make a copy of the filled-in spinner for each pair or small group of students. Model how to use the spinner: Hold a sharpened pencil upright at the center of the spinner. Place the paper clip at the bottom of the pencil. With your fingers, flick the paper clip to use it as a spinner.

Prepare pencils, scissors, and glue for each student. Additionally, provide each pair or small group of students with a pencil and paper clip to use with the spinner.

How to Play

1. Each student gets a Suffix Flip-Book. Each pair or small group of students get a small paper bag with the Base Word Cards and a spinner.
2. Students take turns taking a Base Word Card from the bag.
3. When students get a word card, they glue it to the first blank strip in front of their flip-book.
4. Students then spin the spinner to get a suffix. They then open the flip-book and write the base word with the suffix they spun on the left side of the flip-book. Then they write the meaning of the new word on the right side of the flip-book.
5. Students continue taking turns, repeating steps 2–4, until everyone has filled in their flip-book.

Going Further

- Challenge students to write sentences using the words in their flip-books. Alternatively, they can complete sentence starters, such as the samples below:
  - *The class was cheerful because _____.*
  - *_____ was joyful when _____.*
  - *The kids were fearless when _____.*
- Have students identify synonyms and antonyms.
- For additional practice, make extra copies of the Suffix Flip-Book and Base Word Cards for students to take home.

Base Word Cards

The Ultimate Book of Phonics Word Lists for Grades 3–5 © by Laurie J. Cousseau and Rhonda Graff Scholastic Inc.

_____'s Suffix Flip-Book

fold here ↑

The Ultimate Book of Phonics Word Lists for Grades 3–5 © by Laurie J. Cousseau and Rhonda Graff, Scholastic Inc.

Suffix Spinner

Write the two target suffixes in the spinner below.
Each suffix should appear in two sections.

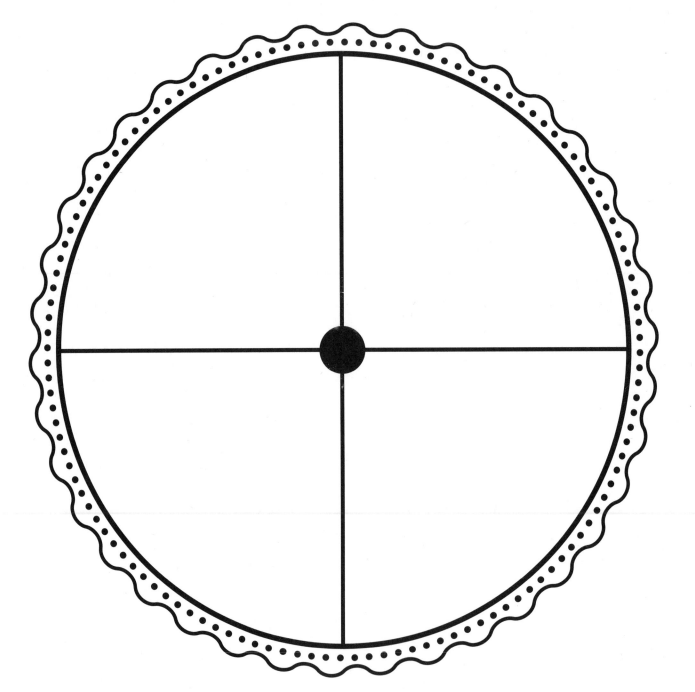

Star Words

This word-building activity is perfect for the whole class, small groups, or independent practice.

You'll Need: Star Words activity sheet (page 116) • pencils

Setting Up the Game

Make a copy of the blank Star Words activity sheet. Decide on a specific root you want students to target (for example, *tract*). Write the target root in the star in the center of the page. Find the corresponding word list in the book and choose words for the activity.

To the left and right side of the star, fill in prefixes and suffixes that can be combined with the root. **Note:** We strongly recommend preplanning. Before filling in the prefixes and suffixes around the star, brainstorm words to see what affixes will allow students to create multiple words using the target root.

Then, make a copy of the activity sheet for each student.

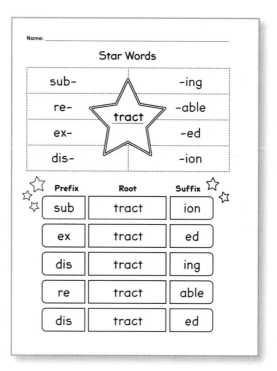

How to Play

1. Students use the root in the star and the prefixes and suffixes around it to make words. They may use only the morphemes on the page. Every word must include the root in the star.

2. Students build words and write them at the bottom of the activity sheet.

3. When students have completed their activity sheet, invite them to share their words.

Going Further

For additional practice, make extra copies of the activity sheet for students to take home and work on with their families. Be sure to fill in the top portion before sending it home.

Name: _____

Star Words

Prefix	Root	Suffix

Match the Meaning

In this vocabulary-boosting activity, students build words and match them to their definitions.

Number of Players: 2

You'll Need: Match the Meaning activity sheet (page 118)
• Prefix & Base/Root Cards and Scoring Spinner (page 119)
• Word Score Sheet (page 120) • scissors • pencil and paper clip
(for the spinner) • pencils

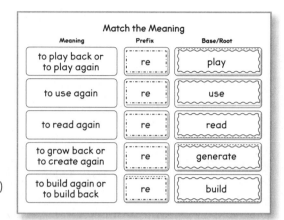

Setting Up the Game

Decide on a prefix you want students to target (for example, *re-*) and find the corresponding word list in the book. Choose five words to highlight for this game. **Note:** Not all words transfer easily from morphemes to word meaning, so plan accordingly.

For instance, *re-* means "again," so *reread* clearly means "to read again." In a word like *retract*, however, it will be more challenging for students to gather meaning without understanding the meaning of *tract*.

Make a copy of the blank Match the Meaning activity sheet. Under the Meaning section, write the definition of each of your five chosen words in a blank box. Then, make a copy of the sheet for each student.

Next, make a copy of the blank Prefix & Base/Root Cards. Using your five chosen words, write one prefix and one base/root in each box. (Be sure to write the prefix in five boxes, one for each word.) Then, make a copy of the sheet for each student and then cut the cards apart. (You can have students cut apart the cards as well.) Detach the Scoring Spinner for use during the game.

For each pair of players, make a copy of the Word Score Sheet. Provide students with pencils to write the words on their score sheet. Model how to use the spinner: Hold a sharpened pencil upright at the center of the spinner. Place the paper clip at the bottom of the pencil. With your fingers, flick the paper clip to use it as a spinner.

How to Play

1. Each player gets their own Match the Meaning activity sheet and set of Prefix & Base/Root Cards. Players share the Word Score Sheet.

2. Players shuffle their word cards and stack them face down next to their activity sheet.

3. Players take turns flipping over one card at a time and placing it in the correct box on their activity sheet. The prefixes all go in the prefix column, but players need to decide where to put the base/root cards by looking at the Meaning column.

4. After players have formed a word completely (the meaning, prefix, and base/root boxes in one row are all filled), they spin the Scoring Spinner to determine how many points they have earned.

5. On their Word Score Sheet, players write their completed word and record how many points they earned for that word.

6. When all the boxes in the Match the Meaning activity sheet have been filled up and all the words are written on the Word Score Sheet, players tally their scores to determine the winner.

Going Further

For additional practice, make extra copies of all the pages for students to take home and play with their families. Be sure to fill in the Meaning section of the Match the Meaning activity sheet before sending it home.

The Ultimate Book of Phonics Word Lists for Grades 3–5 © by Laurie J. Cousseau and Rhonda Graff, Scholastic Inc.

Match the Meaning

Meaning	Prefix	Base/Root

Prefix & Base/Root Cards

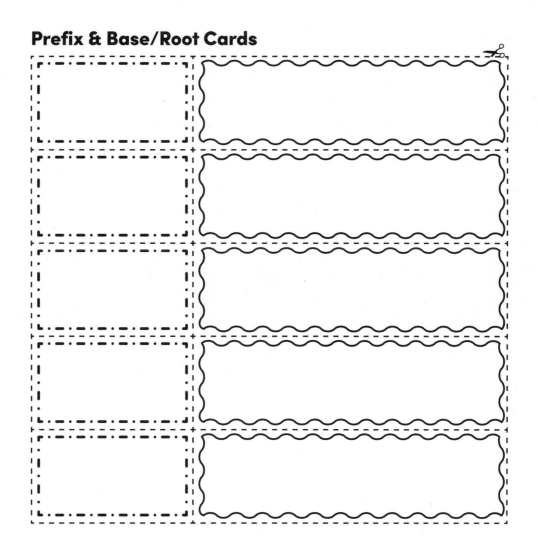

Scoring Spinner

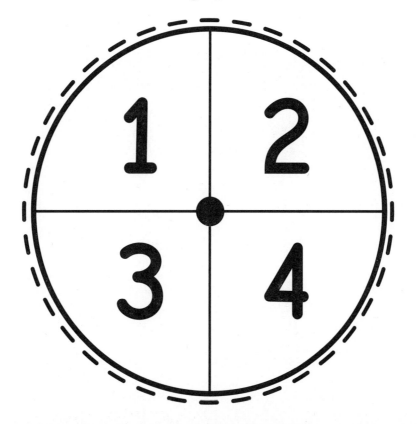

Word Score Sheet

Player 1:	
Word	**Points**
1.	
2.	
3.	
4.	
5.	
Total	

Player 2:	
Word	**Points**
1.	
2.	
3.	
4.	
5.	
Total	

The Ultimate Book of Phonics Word Lists for Grades 3–5 © by Laurie J. Cousseau and Rhonda Graff, Scholastic Inc.

Word Changer

In this activity, students learn that adding a suffix to a word can change its part of speech.

You'll Need: Word Changer activity sheet (page 122) • pencils

Setting Up the Game

Make a copy of the blank Word Changer activity sheet. Decide on a specific suffix you want students to target (for example, -*ment*). Choose a suffix that will change a word's part of speech when added to it (see below for examples). Find the corresponding word list in the book and choose words for the game. Write the suffix in the center column of the handout. On the left side, write the part of speech and the base words. On the right side, fill in the part of speech and leave the rest of the box blank. Then make a copy of the sheet for each student.

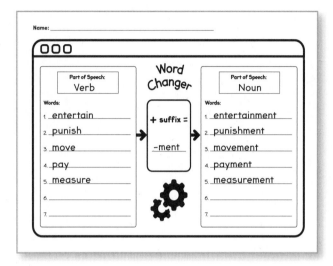

Suffixes that change a base word's part of speech:

-*al* (noun ➔ adjective)	-*al* (verb ➔ noun)
season ➔ seasonal	survive ➔ survival
nation ➔ national	refuse ➔ refusal
coast ➔ coastal	
-*ion* (verb ➔ noun)	-*y* (noun ➔ adjective)
construct ➔ construction	cloud ➔ cloudy
direct ➔ direction	chill ➔ chilly
exhaust ➔ exhaustion	dream ➔ dreamy

How to Play

1. Students fill in the Word Changer activity sheet, noting how adding the suffix changes the word's part of speech. Students should verbally explain to a teacher/classmate what is happening; for example, "*Entertain* is a verb, but when we add the suffix -*ment* to it, it becomes a noun." For each entry, they should discuss the meaning of the suffix and of the original word and the new word.

2. On the back of the sheet, students should write sentences using the words, noting how the words are used in the sentences. Discuss and share the sentences.

Going Further

- Create charts that show how the suffixes create new words and change the part of speech. Then, help students become more aware of these words in everyday speech.

- For additional practice, make extra copies of the activity sheet for students to take home and work on with their families. Be sure to provide a suffix and related words before copying the page.

Name: _____

Word Changer

Part of Speech:

Words:

1. _____
2. _____
3. _____
4. _____
5. _____
6. _____
7. _____

+ suffix =

_____

Part of Speech:

Words:

1. _____
2. _____
3. _____
4. _____
5. _____
6. _____
7. _____

Bucket Sort

Students sort words into their respective buckets according to parts of speech.

You'll Need: Bucket Sort activity sheet (page 124) • scissors • pencils • glue (optional)

Setting Up the Game

Make a copy of the blank Bucket Sort activity sheet. Decide what suffix you want students to target (for example, *-ion*). Find the corresponding word list in the book and choose words for the game. **Note:** Although this activity is set up for sorting parts of speech, it is very versatile and can be used for sorting various morphemes or any spelling pattern or concept that can be contrasted with one another.

Fill in the categories on top of each bucket (for example, "verbs" and "nouns"). On the right-hand side of the activity sheet, fill in words that fit into the two categories. Make sure all the words fit into the two categories. Make a copy of the filled-in activity sheet for each student.

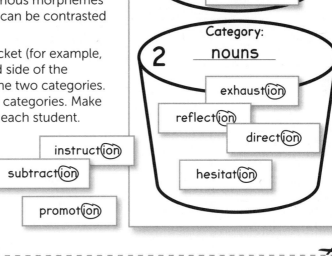

Name: _____

Bucket Sort

Category:

1 verbs

exhaust
reflect
hesitate
instruct
promote   direct
subtract

Category:

2 nouns

exhaustion
reflection
direction
instruction
subtraction
hesitation
promotion

How to Play

1. Students cut out all the words on the right-hand side of the activity page.

2. Students read the words and circle any suffixes.

3. Students read the category titles on the buckets. Then they sort the words into the two categories. They can glue the words to the buckets.

4. It is important to follow up the activity with questioning and discussion. For example, you might ask: *What happens to a word when you add the suffix -ion?*

5. Encourage students to use the words in sentences.

Going Further

For additional practice, make extra copies of the activity sheet for students to take home and work on with their families.

Bucket Sort

Category:

1 _____

Category:

2 _____

Word Towers

Players claim Word Towers by reading the words in each Tower and using each word in a sentence. They then define the words, using their knowledge of morphology.

Number of Players: 2

You'll Need: Word Towers game board (page 127) • Word Definition Chart (page 128) • Tower Spinner (page 129) • pencil and paper clip (for the spinner) • scissors • different-colored pencils

Setting Up the Game

Make a copy of the blank Word Towers game board sheet. (**Note:** The sheet has two identical game boards: one on the top half of the page and the other on the bottom half. Fill in the top and bottom halves exactly the same.) Choose three morphemes (roots or affixes) you want students to

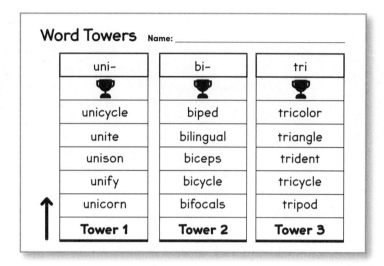

target (for example, *uni-*, *bi-*, and *tri-*). Write them at the top of the Towers above the trophies. Find the corresponding word lists in the book and choose words for the game. Write one word in each space of the corresponding Towers. Make sure the top and bottom halves of the game board are identical. Make a copy of the completed game board and then cut it in half, one half for each player.

Make a copy of the Word Definition Chart. In the first column, write the words that are on the Towers. Decide what words to include on the list; not all words need to be included. Students will use their knowledge of morphemes to write each word's definition in the second column. Encourage students to look up unknown words. You may want to provide definitions if the morphemes don't align directly with the meanings.

Make a copy of the Tower Spinner page for each pair of players and provide them with a pencil and paper clip to use as a spinner. Model how to use the spinner: Hold a sharpened pencil upright at the center of the spinner. Place the paper clip at the bottom of the pencil. With your fingers, flick the paper clip to use it as a spinner. The bottom of the spinner page includes space to record the winner of each Tower and the ultimate winner.

Provide each player with a different-colored pencil.

How to Play

1. Before playing, introduce the morphemes featured in the game to students. Students could also try to decipher the meaning of the morphemes based on the words listed.

2. Players take turns spinning the spinner. Each number matches a Tower.

   • If the spinner lands on 1, the player reads the first word on Tower 1 (starting at the bottom) and uses the word in a sentence. Then the player colors in that word.

   • If the spinner lands on 2, the player does the same with the first word from Tower 2, and so on.

   • Remember to start at the bottom and work toward the top of each Tower. On the spinner, players may also skip a turn, take an extra turn, or choose a word from a Tower of their choice.

3. When a player colors in all the words on a Tower and reaches the trophy at the top, that player claims that Tower. The player must reread the words and sign their initials on the spinner page next to the corresponding Tower.

4. Play continues until someone wins the next Tower. The player who wins two out of three Towers is the Ultimate Champion.

5. After the Towers have been claimed, students can work on defining the words on their Word Definition Chart, using their knowledge of morphology and any other resource available.

Going Further

• Challenge students to look for other words that have the same morphemes.

• For additional practice, make extra copies of the game board and related sheets for students to take home and play with their families.

The Ultimate Book of Phonics Word Lists for Grades 3–5 © by Laurie J. Cousseau and Rhonda Graff, Scholastic Inc.

Word Towers   Name: _____

🏆	🏆	🏆
Tower 1	**Tower 2**	**Tower 3**

↑

Word Towers   Name: _____

🏆	🏆	🏆
Tower 1	**Tower 2**	**Tower 3**

↑

Word Definition Chart

Word	Definition

Tower Spinner

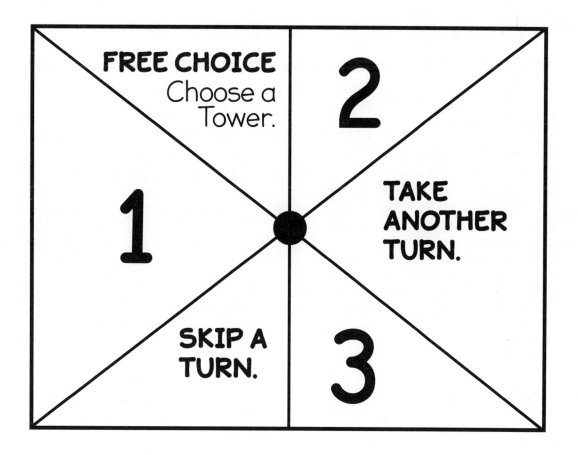

	Player's Initials
Tower 1 Champion	
Tower 2 Champion	
Tower 3 Champion	
Ultimate Champion	

Body of Words Game

In this fun game, players identify words with roots related to different parts of the body—and then draw those parts on the human figure on the game board.

Number of Players: 2

You'll Need: Body Word Cards (pages 131, 134) • Body of Words game board (pages 132–133) • scissors • glue • pencils • file folder (optional)

Setting Up the Game

Make a copy of the blank Body of Words game board. To assemble the game board, fold or cut along the dotted line (B), and tape (B) to (A) as indicated. (Optional: Glue or tape the game board to the inside of a file folder to make it sturdier.) The purpose of this game is to introduce root words related to the body in a fun way by "building" a body.

Make a copy of the Body Word Cards and cut them apart. These cards feature words with roots related to specific parts of the body. Find other related words on the word lists in the book if you want to add more or change the cards for additional play. Shuffle the Body Word Cards and stack them face down next to the game board.

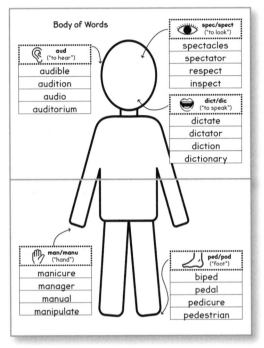

How to Play

1. Players take turns picking a Body Word Card, underlining the root, and placing it in the box next to the part of the body related to that root. For example, *audible* goes in the box labeled *aud*, next to the ear.

2. After putting the word card in its corresponding box, players draw a related body part on the human figure on the game board. For example, if they picked the *audible* card, players draw an ear on the human figure.

3. Players continue taking turns until all the Body Word Cards have been read with their roots underlined and body parts have been drawn on the figure.

4. When all the Body Word Cards are in the boxes, players work together to choose four words to write in each box. They can then study the words further: What does each word mean? How is the root related to its meaning?

Going Further

- Challenge players to look for other words that have the same morphemes.
- For additional practice, make extra copies of the game board and related sheets for students to take home and play with their families.

The Ultimate Book of Phonics Word Lists for Grades 3–5 © by Laurie J. Cousseau and Rhonda Graff, Scholastic Inc.

Body Word Cards

audible	audition	audio
auditorium	audiovisual	audit
auditor	auditory	audience
audiology	dictate	dictator
diction	contradict	dictionary
predict	verdict	perspective
spectacles	speculate	spectator

Body of Words

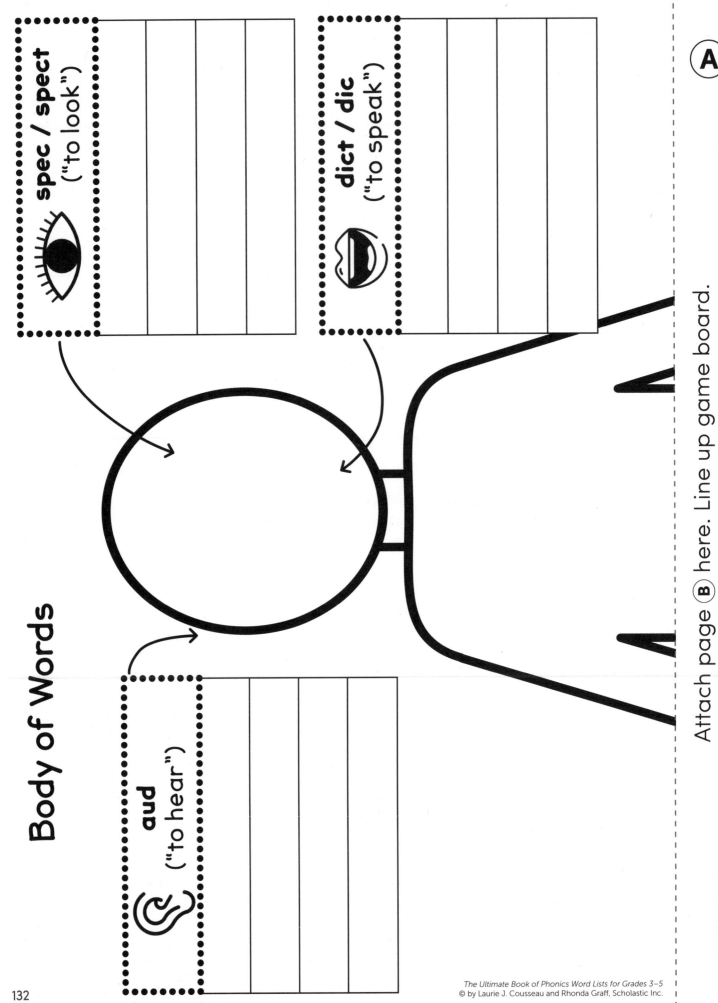

spec / spect ("to look")

dict / dic ("to speak")

aud ("to hear")

Attach page Ⓑ here. Line up game board.

The Ultimate Book of Phonics Word Lists for Grades 3–5
© by Laurie J. Cousseau and Rhonda Graff, Scholastic Inc.

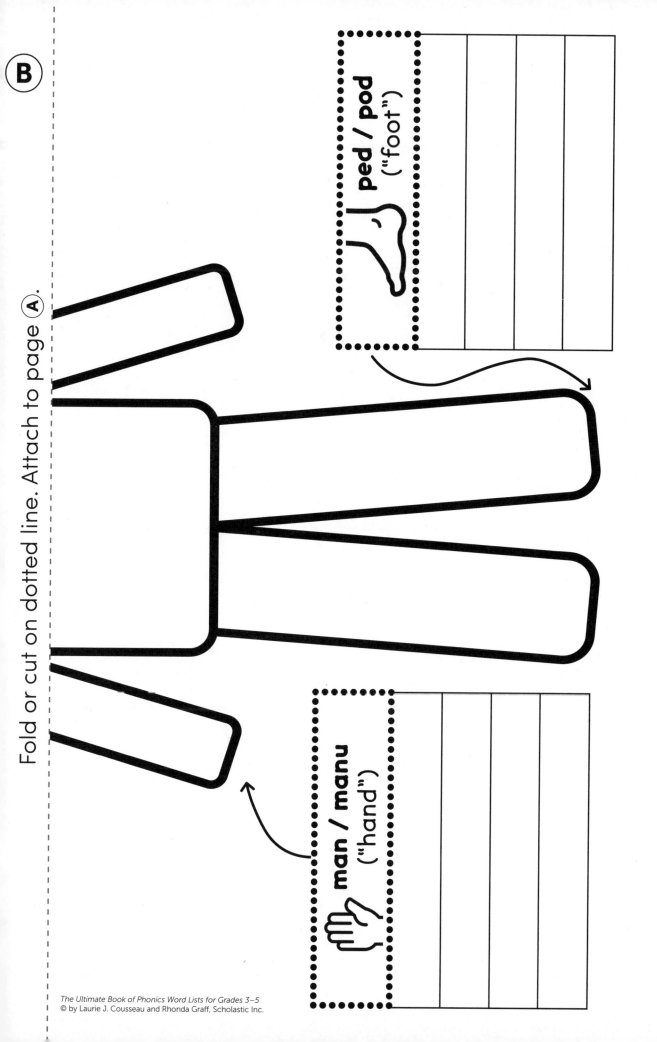

Ⓑ

Fold or cut on dotted line. Attach to page **Ⓐ**.

ped / pod
("foot")

man / manu
("hand")

Body Word Cards continued

respect	inspect	manifest
manager	manicure	manipulate
manual	manuscript	manufacture
biped	centipede	pedal
peddler	pedestrian	pedicure
quadruped	podiatrist	tripod

The Ultimate Book of Phonics Word Lists for Grades 3–5 © by Laurie J. Cousseau and Rhonda Graff, Scholastic Inc.

Build-a-Word Game

Word-building is super fun with this game in which players go around the board to collect Prefix, Suffix, and Base/Root Cards. Then, they build words out of the cards they collected. The player who builds the most words wins!

Number of Players: 2 to 4

You'll Need: Word Combinations List (page 137) • Build-a-Word Game Board (pages 138–139) • Prefix Cards and Suffix Cards (page 140) • Base/Root Cards (page 141) • Bonus Cards (page 142) • Word-Building Mat (page 143) • game pieces (e.g., buttons) • die • file folder (optional)

Setting Up the Game

Make a copy of the Build-a-Word game board. To assemble the game board, fold or cut along the dotted line (B), and tape (B) to (A) as indicated. (Optional: Glue or tape the game board to the inside of a file folder to make it sturdier.) **Note:** The completed game board template is generic and may be used with various Prefix, Base/Root, and Suffix cards.

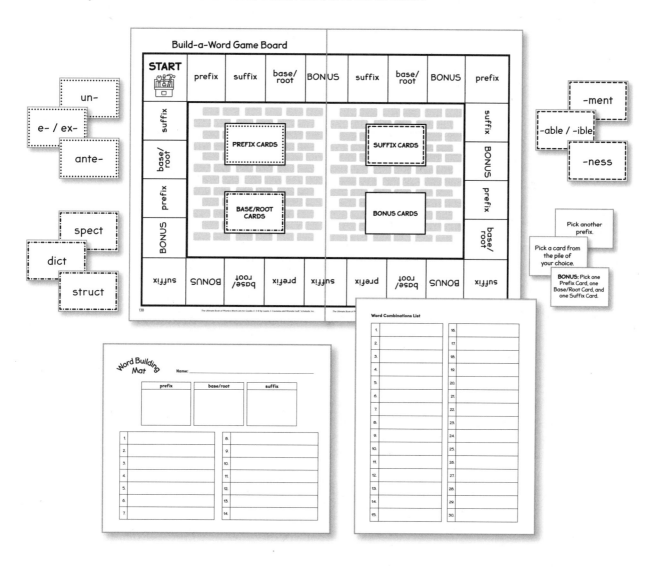

Make a copy of the blank Prefix Cards and Suffix Cards and the blank Base/Root Cards. Decide on the prefixes, suffixes, and base/roots you want students to focus on. **Note:** We strongly recommend preplanning and choosing the base/roots first and then using the word lists in the book to create a rough-draft list of possible words for the game. Then, look at that list for common prefixes and suffixes to include in the game. Write the prefixes and suffixes on the blank Prefix Cards and Suffix Cards. You can write each affix more than once. Then write the corresponding base/roots on the Base/Roots Cards. After you finalize the prefixes, suffixes, and base/roots that will be included in the game, write all possible word combinations on the Word Combination List page. This list of all possible combinations using the given prefixes, suffixes, and base/roots will be used as a self-checking answer key for students.

Helpful Hint: Preplanning is essential. When planning for the game, the teacher is actually taking a whole word and deconstructing it into its parts: prefixes, suffixes, base/roots. When playing the game, students are constructing words by taking these individual parts and combining them to build new words.

Make two or three copies of the Prefix Cards and Suffix Cards and the Base/Root Cards. Cut them apart, putting the Prefix Cards, the Suffix Cards, and the Base/Root Cards in their own groups. These will provide ample cards to build words.

Make one copy of the Bonus Cards and cut them apart. Shuffle them and stack them next to the game board.

Make a copy of the Word-Building Mat for each player. Provide each player with a game piece and pencil and provide each group of players with a die.

How to Play

1. Place the game board between the players. Shuffle the Prefix Cards and stack them face down on the game board where indicated. Do the same for the Suffix Cards, the Base/Root Cards, and the Bonus Cards.

2. Players place their game pieces on START. Players take turns rolling the die and moving around the board accordingly.

3. If players land on a prefix space, they pick a Prefix Card. If they land on a suffix space, they pick a Suffix Card. They do the same for Base/Root Cards and Bonus Cards.

4. If players get a Bonus Card, they follow the instructions on the card.

5. Players work their way around the board collecting cards. Players can decide whether to go around the board once, twice, or more, depending on how many cards they collect.

6. After all the cards have been collected, players use their Word-Building Mats to build words with the cards they collected. They can only build words with the cards they collected. The player who builds the most words wins. (**Note:** Players can check their completed words against the Word Combinations List.)

Going Further

- Encourage students to explore morphemes further. Guide their exploration with these questions: *What do the morphemes mean? How do the word parts work together to create meaning? What additional words can you build?*

- For additional practice, make extra copies of the Build-a-Word game board and related sheets for students to take home and play with their families.

The Ultimate Book of Phonics Word Lists for Grades 3–5 © by Laurie J. Cousseau and Rhonda Graff, Scholastic Inc.

Word Combinations List

1.	
2.	
3.	
4.	
5.	
6.	
7.	
8.	
9.	
10.	
11.	
12.	
13.	
14.	
15.	

16.	
17.	
18.	
19.	
20.	
21.	
22.	
23.	
24.	
25.	
26.	
27.	
28.	
29.	
30.	

Build-a-Word Game Board

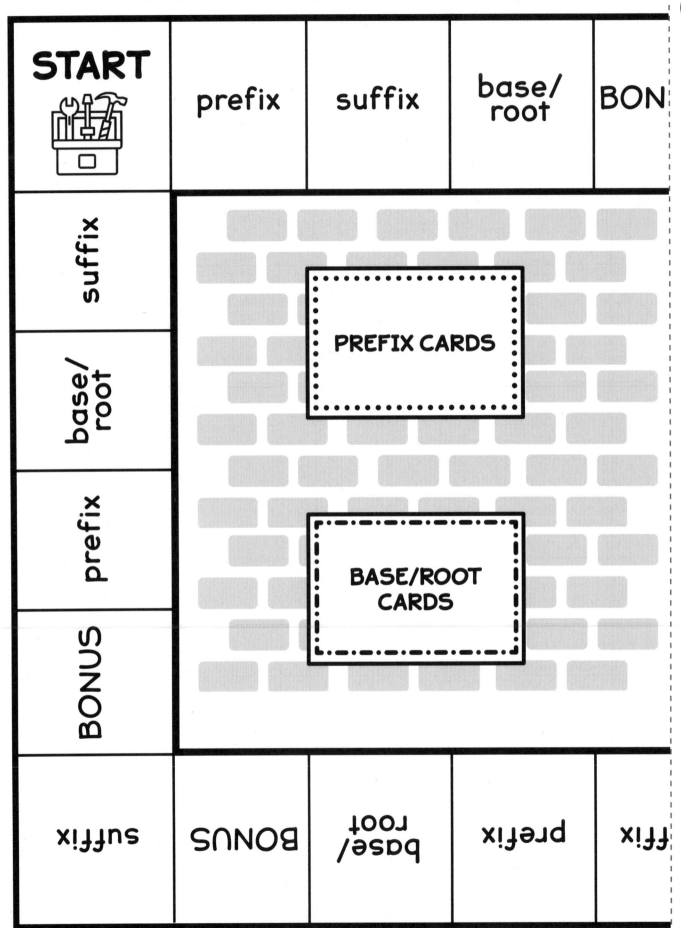

START

prefix

suffix

base/root

BON

suffix

base/root

prefix

BONUS

PREFIX CARDS

BASE/ROOT CARDS

suffix

BONUS

base/root

prefix

ffix

Attach page Ⓑ here. Line up game board.

US | suffix | base/root | BONUS | prefix

Fold or cut on dotted line. Attach to page (A).

suffix

BONUS

prefix

base/root

SUFFIX CARDS

BONUS CARDS

ns | prefix | base/root | BONUS | suffix

Prefix and Suffix Cards

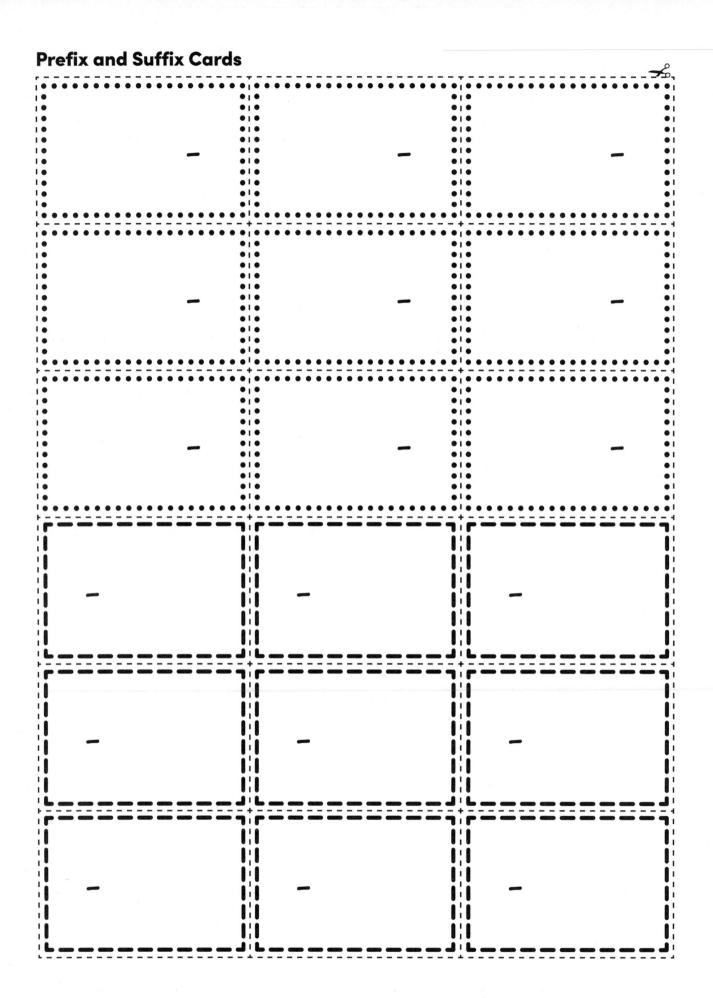

The Ultimate Book of Phonics Word Lists for Grades 3–5 © by Laurie J. Cousseau and Rhonda Graff, Scholastic Inc.

Base/Root Cards

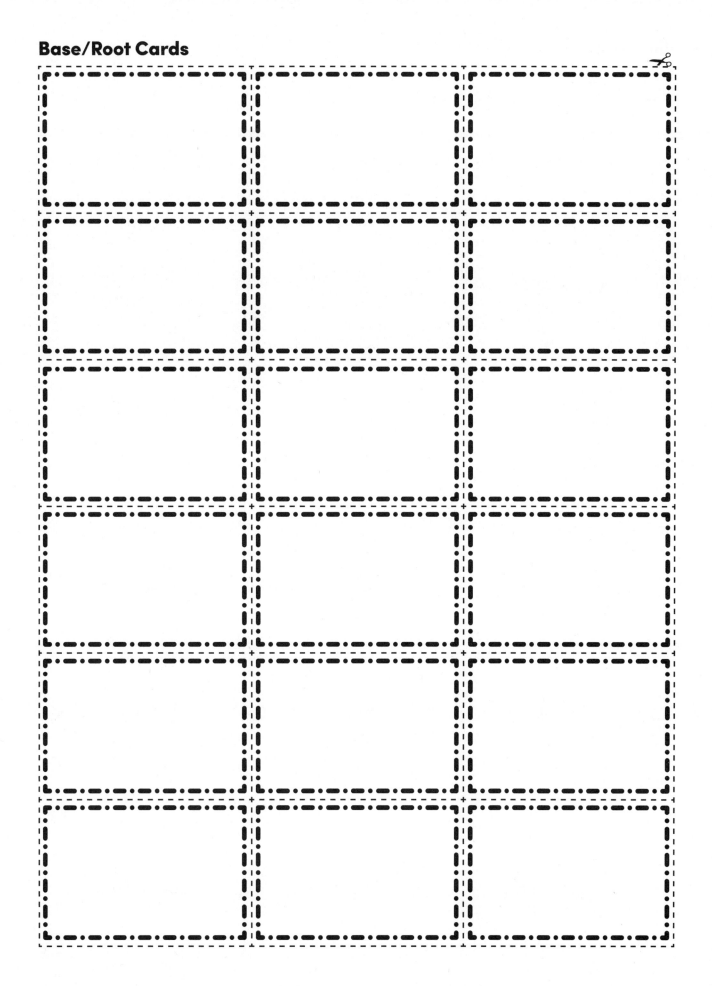

Bonus Cards

Pick another prefix.	Pick another suffix.	Pick another base/root.
Pick a card from the pile of your choice.	Go back three spaces.	Go ahead two spaces.
Go back two spaces.	Take a card from your opponent.	Make a trade with your opponent.
BONUS: Pick one Prefix Card, one Base/Root Card, and one Suffix Card.	**BONUS:** Pick one Prefix Card, one Base/Root Card, and one Suffix Card.	**BONUS:** Pick one Prefix Card, one Base/Root Card, and one Suffix Card.
Pick two Prefix Cards.	Pick two Suffix Cards.	Pick two Base/Root Cards.
Take a card from your opponent.	Make a trade with your opponent.	Pick two cards of your choice.

The Ultimate Book of Phonics Word Lists for Grades 3–5 © by Laurie J. Cousseau and Rhonda Graff, Scholastic Inc.

The Ultimate Book of Phonics Word Lists for Grades 3–5 © by Laurie J. Cousseau and Rhonda Graff, Scholastic Inc.

Word-Building Mat

Name: _____

Prefix	Base/Root	Suffix

1.
2.
3.
4.
5.
6.
7.

8.
9.
10.
11.
12.
13.
14.

Extra Cards

The Ultimate Book of Phonics Word Lists for Grades 3–5 © by Laurie J. Cousseau and Rhonda Graff, Scholastic Inc.